—— The Best of the Best ——

PANINI PRESS
COOKBOOK

Brimming with creative inspiration, how-to projects, and useful information to enrich your everyday life, Quarto Knows is a favorite destination for those pursuing their interests and passions. Visit our site and dig deeper with our books into your area of interest: Quarto Creates, Quarto Cooks, Quarto Homes, Quarto Lives, Quarto Drives, Quarto Explores, Quarto Gifts, or Quarto Kids.

First Published in 2019 by The Harvard Common Press, an imprint of The Quarto Group, 100 Cummings Center, Suite 265-D, Beverly, MA 01915, USA.
T (978) 282-9590 F (978) 283-2742 QuartoKnows.com

The Harvard Common Press titles are also available at discount for retail, wholesale, promotional, and bulk purchase. For details, contact the Special Sales Manager by email at specialsales@quarto.com or by mail at The Quarto Group, Attn: Special Sales Manager, 100 Cummings Center, Suite 265-D, Beverly, MA 01915, USA.

23 22 21 20 19   1 2 3 4 5

ISBN: 978-1-55832-961-4

Digital edition published in 2019

Content in this book originally appeared in *The Ultimate Panini Press Cookbook* by Kathy Strahs (The Harvard Common Press, 2013)

Design and Page Layout: Sporto
Food Photography: Ellen Callaway | www.CallawayPhoto.com; Except for front matter and page 85
Food Styling: Joy Howard | joyfoodstyle.com

Printed in China

The Best of the Best

PANINI PRESS
COOKBOOK

100

Surefire Recipes for Making Panini—and Many
Other Things—on Your Panini Press or Other
Countertop Grill

Kathy Strahs

HARVARD
COMMON
PRESS

CONTENTS

PREFACE

When *The Ultimate Panini Press Cookbook* by Kathy Strahs was first published in 2013, there were several books available on panini sandwiches but none about the entire range of things—panini included, but so much more—that you could make on a panini press. Kathy brilliantly showed how all manner of countertop grills, from panini presses to "griddlers" to "electric indoor grills," could make all kinds of foods besides panini, including grilled cheese sandwiches, burgers and cheesesteaks, grilled meats for salads, and even desserts. The book has gone on to become the best-selling book on panini and on indoor grilling generally.

In this volume you will find a curated selection of one hundred of the best recipes from Kathy's groundbreaking book, presented now with new photographs and in a new design. We hope these recipes make you love your panini press even more than you already do and that they help you get delectable meals on the table quickly and easily.

—The Editors of the Harvard Common Press

PANINI and PANINI PRESSES
THE BASICS

Panini Presses—The Ins and Outs

The panini press is, of course, named for the Italian pressed sandwiches that have become so popular here in recent years. You will sometimes see a panini press called simply a "sandwich maker" or an "indoor grill." For the purposes of this book, when I say "panini press" I'm referring to any countertop appliance—including a George Foreman grill—that can heat food between two grates.

That said, as with any appliance, not all panini presses are the same. Some come with a myriad of features and are large enough to accommodate a family's worth of steaks, while others are very basic and designed to fit comfortably in a college dorm room. They're available at all price points, ranging from as little as $20 for a very simple model with a single heat setting to upwards of $300 for one with an LCD screen and removable plates.

People often ask me which type of panini press I recommend. My response is usually "Well, what do you plan to use it for?" I suggest examining five key features to help you determine which panini press meets your needs and your budget:
- Adjustable thermostat
- Grill surface area
- Drainage
- Removable plates
- Adjustable height control

ADJUSTABLE THERMOSTAT

An adjustable thermostat allows you to control the amount of heat you're grilling with. Some panini presses allow you to set a specific cooking temperature (350°F [180°C or gas mark 4], for example); some come with "high," "medium," and "low" settings; some give an adjustable range between "panini" and "sear"; and others are built with a simple on/off switch and no ability to adjust the heat level at all.

If you're planning to grill mainly sandwiches, a panini press without an adjustable thermostat will likely suit your needs. However, the ability to control the temperature is key when grilling certain foods. For my Grilled Rib-Eye Steak (page 93), for instance, I turn the heat up high to get a nice, crusty sear on the meat. To slowly render the fat and crisp the skin on my Grilled Duck Breasts (page 47), I use a medium-low setting.

In general, the more heating options, the more expensive the panini press will be. You can buy a press without an adjustable thermostat for as little as $20 or $30; presses with adjustable thermostats typically cost $70 and up.

GRILL SURFACE AREA

Some folks prefer a smaller grill due to space constraints in their kitchen or dorm room, or if there are just one or two people in the household. Small grills are also more portable, making them a great option for those who like to bring their panini press on vacation. A large grill surface area is especially beneficial to those who want to make a lot of panini or other foods for a whole family at once—it can be a real time-saver not to have to cook in batches.

Panini presses with large surface areas, accommodating four panini or more, are pricier than small models and usually offer other premium features. They typically range between $70 and $300.

DRAINAGE

If you plan to use your panini press to grill meats, poultry, and other foods beyond panini, it's important to choose a press with drainage features. The grill plates on many panini presses and other indoor grills are designed to drain excess fat, which can make them a healthier cooking alternative. On some models, you can adjust the plates to tilt forward to allow the fat to flow into a drip pan, while others remain flat and drain via the back of the grill.

Some no-frills panini presses do not have any drainage features at all—you'll notice that the lower plate stays flat and there are no cutouts or sloped edges to allow fat to roll away. Models like these are intended mainly for grilling panini and shouldn't be used for raw meats.

FEATURE COMPARISON

You'll find panini presses on the market with features and price points to suit all needs. Here is a rundown of what you can expect to find at the basic, midrange, and premium levels of the panini press spectrum.

BASIC ($20–$50)

Pros: Compact size; cooks quickly; affordable

Cons: No adjustable thermostat, drainage feature, removable plates, or adjustable height control; small to medium grill surface area; may not be suitable for grilling raw meats (refer to the manufacturer's instructions)

MIDRANGE ($50–$80)

Pros: May have an adjustable thermostat and drainage feature; larger grill surface area; greater grilling versatility, including raw meats

Cons: Not likely to have removable plates or adjustable height control

PREMIUM ($80–$300)

Pros: Adjustable thermostat; large grill surface area, with drainage feature; may have removable plates; may have adjustable height control; greatest grilling versatility

Cons: Requires more counter space; less portable; less affordable

REMOVABLE PLATES

Melted and cooked-on bits are a fact of life with the panini press. If your grill has removable plates, cleanup is much easier. You can just pop off the plates and scrub them in the sink or dishwasher. But if your grill doesn't have removable plates, don't despair—I've got helpful cleaning tips for you on page 11.

ADJUSTABLE HEIGHT CONTROL

I regularly use the adjustable height control feature on my panini press to give me greater flexibility in terms of the types of foods I can grill. This feature allows me to position the upper plate to hover above open-faced sandwiches, make very light contact with soft foods like tomatoes and French toast, and regulate the amount of pressure applied to the panini so that the ingredients don't squeeze out. Most panini presses come with a floating hinge, which allows for a degree of pressure control, but very few offer fully adjustable height control.

Whether your panini press comes with all of these features or just one or two, nearly any model will make grilling sandwiches and other foods an easy task.

How to Use a Panini Press

Most panini presses are very easy and straightforward to operate. Here are my tips for getting the best results when it comes to heating, grilling, and cleaning.

HEATING

Each panini press model heats differently—some you just plug in, while others have specific heat settings. As you can imagine, this poses quite a challenge for me when it comes to developing recipes that each of you can accurately follow with whichever type of panini press you might have. "High" on one grill might be "sear" on another, and still others have no option to set a heat level at all.

For the vast majority of the recipes in this cookbook, I've suggested setting your panini press to "medium-high" heat. That's a level that's not the highest, but not the lowest—somewhere in between, leaning toward the higher side. (Note: Panini presses with simple on/off heating tend to run on the hotter side, so your cooking time may be shorter with these machines.) The good news is that, for most recipes, the exact temperature won't really matter. Just look at the food you're grilling and decide whether it looks done to you or not. If it's a meat dish, I highly recommend using a meat thermometer (see more discussion on meat thermometers on page 19) to monitor doneness.

GRILLING

Notice that I called this section "Grilling." I didn't call it "Flattening" or "Leaning Into the Panini Press to Make Sure the Sandwich Gets Good and Flat." I'm not sure where the practice of pressing down hard on a panini press originated. I see evidence of it over and over again in photos, but it's not what I'd recommend unless you happen to like really flat food. Today's panini presses are designed to provide the right degree of pressure, without any need for you to press down—or flatten—your food.

My recommendation, whether you're making sandwiches or other foods, is that you *grill* them. That is, you place the food on the grates, close the lid so that it's resting on top of the food, and wait until it's done. If you're grilling panini, the sound of melted cheese sizzling on the grates is a good indication that it's time to take the panini off the grill. For meats, I always use a meat thermometer that beeps when the desired temperature has been reached.

CLEANING

As I've mentioned before, if your panini press comes with removable plates, cleanup is relatively easy. Once the grill has cooled down, you just unsnap the grates from the base and wash them in the sink or dishwasher. But what about grills without removable plates? Truth be told, the grill I use most often doesn't have removable plates. No big deal—here's how I get it as clean as new.

SCRAPE IT WHILE IT'S HOT. More often than not there's melted cheese remaining on the grates after I've grilled panini. It comes with the territory. Thanks to the nonstick coating on the grates, cheese scrapes off easily with the help of the plastic grill scraper that came with my panini press (if yours didn't come with its own grill scraper, see my recommendation for a silicone grill brush on page 22) and a clean cloth. For more stubborn stuck-on food—which often happens when I grill meat, especially with sweet marinades—I unplug the grill and, while it's still hot, I (very carefully) try to loosen and lift off as many bits as possible with the grill scraper. Then I let the grill cool completely. *Safety note:* Make sure the unplugged power cord is resting next to the grill, not dangling where it could accidentally be pulled and drag the panini press off the table or counter. And never use an abrasive pad on the grill as it may damage the nonstick coating.

TAKE IT TO THE SINK. Once the grill has cooled, I bring it over to the counter adjacent to the kitchen sink (let me reiterate—the grill *must be unplugged* before you bring it anywhere near water). I position the grill so that the front edge is just above the bowl of the sink. Then I squirt on some dish soap and wash the lower plate with a wet sponge and use a silicone grill brush to get to those hidden places between the grates. Once it's clean, I use the pull-out faucet to rinse off the plate and then dry it with paper towels (just in case I missed any bits of blackened cooked-on food that would stain my nice kitchen towels). If your sink doesn't have a pull-out faucet, you can also rinse with a very wet sponge. *Safety note:* As with all electrical appliances, don't ever let the electrical connection get wet and *never* submerge any part of the panini press itself in water.

TURN IT UPSIDE DOWN. And what about that upper plate, you ask? Cleaning that had been a challenge for me until I discovered an easy solution—I turn the entire machine on its end so that the upper plate lies flat on the counter over the sink. Then I can clean it just as I did with the lower plate. Just be aware that with this new distribution of weight—the upper plate is typically much lighter than the lower plate—the press may be less stable, so work carefully.

REMEMBER THE DRIP TRAY. Some panini presses come equipped with a drip tray that is so well concealed that it's easy to forget about it. Especially after grilling meats and vegetables, it's important to clean out any fat or juices that may have accumulated.

Ingredients for Perfect Panini

"You don't have to cook fancy or complicated masterpieces—just good food from fresh ingredients."
—Julia Child

BREAD

Bread, the traditional foundation of most panini, can take many forms—loaf slices, rolls, baguettes, flatbreads, and so on. When I'm deciding which type of bread to use for a sandwich, I take a lot into consideration:

- Will my fillings hold up well on sliced bread, or will I need something more substantial, like a baguette?
- Do I want the bread itself to contribute flavor to the sandwich—such as with an olive or rosemary bread—or should it play more of a neutral supporting role?
- Are there specific breads that match the cultural heritage of my sandwich, such as a *telera* roll for a Mexican torta or ciabatta for a sandwich with lots of Italian meats?
- What kind of bread do I have in my house at this moment?

Choice of bread can have a real impact on the structure, texture, and flavor of your panini. Often it's easiest just to use what you happen to have on hand, but to get the very best results when grilling sandwiches, here are some thoughts to keep in mind.

KEEP IT DENSE (MOSTLY). Generally speaking, denser bread is best when it comes to grilling panini. Throughout this book you'll see me suggesting that you use rustic breads "sliced from a dense bakery loaf." This isn't me just being all fancy-pants food snob (for the most part). There is a practical reason that I specify denser bread and advocate slicing it yourself. Dense bread—such as the freeform loaves you find in the bakery section of your grocery store—will hold its shape better than soft, pre-sliced sandwich bread when it gets between the two grates (see the photo on page 14).

Now, with every rule, there is an exception: I do use softer breads from time to time. Two examples are my Brie, Nutella, and Basil Panini (page 159), which is grilled on brioche, and my Caramel Apple-Stuffed French Toast (page 154), which calls for challah. In these instances, I cut the slices extra-thick to accommodate some compression during grilling. They still retain some of their airiness, which I want in these recipes. So if you're an especially big fan of softer breads and really want to grill with them, I'd advise cutting thicker slices.

THE BAKERY LOAF VS. SLICED SANDWICH BREAD

I grilled the sandwich on the left on a country *levain* from my local grocery store. I sliced the bread myself, about ½ inch (1.3 cm) thick. As you can see, the bread maintained its thickness, for the most part, and didn't get soggy. On the right is the same sandwich grilled on regular pre-sliced sandwich bread. The soft, airy bread—which is normally very desirable for cold sandwiches—flattened to nearly a cracker. The weight of the panini press plates is simply too much for softer breads. Dense is the way to go.

THINK OUTSIDE THE BREAD. We tend to focus on the fillings that go inside the sandwich, but for the best sandwiches you should flavor the outside as well.

In many panini recipes throughout this book, you'll see that I call for spreading butter or olive oil on the outside of the bread prior to assembly. Your sandwich will come out fine if you omit this step—it's not required to prevent sticking, as most panini presses have a nonstick coating on the grates—but a little swipe of butter or oil will add flavor and a bit of crunch to the bread, as well as more defined grill marks (which are a nice aesthetic touch).

Another way to flavor the outside of the bread is through crusting. You can crumble all sorts of different foods—tortilla chips, nuts, and cookies, to name a few—and mix them with softened butter to create spreads that will turn into crunchy, flavorful crusts on the outside of your sandwiches when they're grilled. See my Honey Walnut–Crusted Aged Cheddar Panini (page 136), and Granola-Crusted Pear, Almond Butter, and Honey Panini (page 147) for examples of these crusts in action.

VENTURE BEYOND THE BAGUETTE. Lastly, I encourage you to think beyond the traditional types of breads that we use for sandwiches and play around with other creative options: pound cake, banana bread, tortillas, zucchini bread, corn bread—whatever you can possibly "sandwich." After a while, nearly everything in your fridge and pantry will start looking like a great candidate for grilling on your panini press!

MEAT

The meats I typically use for panini fall into three categories: deli, leftovers, and panini-grilled.

DELI MEATS. Good-quality sliced deli meats are often the most convenient meats to use in panini. You can buy anything from turkey to roast beef to prosciutto presliced and packaged in any grocery store. However, I've found that it's usually less expensive to grab a number at the deli counter and have the butcher slice exactly the amount I need.

LEFTOVERS. My mother-in-law taught me to appreciate the versatility of leftovers. With a little creativity, you can transform leftovers into a new dish that will rival—and just might outshine—the original. Especially around the holidays, when we tend to cook larger roasts, it's a great time to pull out the panini press and start reinventing. Throughout this cookbook I've highlighted recipes that are particularly suitable for repurposing the cooked chicken, turkey, beef, lamb, and pork you already have on hand.

PANINI-GRILLED MEATS. Depending on the grill you own (see the Feature Comparison box on page 10), you can often use it to prepare your fillings as well as the sandwiches themselves! It takes just a few minutes to grill chicken breasts or steak that you can then build into panini. In most cases you will want to unplug the panini press, cool it, and clean the grates between grilling the meat and grilling the sandwiches. The time isn't wasted, however, because your meat needs a chance to rest anyway.

CHEESE

I grill panini with all types of cheese. Of course, I go for the easy melters most often—cheddar, mozzarella, and Gruyère are among my favorites. But I also choose cheeses like feta, blue cheese, and goat cheese, whose intense flavor more than makes up for their lack of meltability.

Explore the cheese shops in your area or get to know the folks in the cheese department at your local grocery store. They can often introduce you to interesting cheeses.

FRUITS AND VEGETABLES

Before I started grilling panini on a regular basis, the fruits and vegetables I used on my sandwiches were largely limited to lettuce, tomatoes, onions, and occasionally preserves. I still use those ingredients, of course, but far more garden and orchard treats make their way onto my bread these days.

SLICED VS. SHREDDED

I've gone back and forth between sliced and shredded cheese for panini. I use both forms, but the best approach I've found is slicing cheese thinly by hand with a cheese slicer (see page 20). Here's why:

PRE-SLICED CHEESE

Pros: It's the most convenient. You can buy a wide variety of pre-sliced cheese, and the slices are ready to go.

Cons: It can take a while for thick pre-sliced cheese to melt, sometimes too long. The bread may start to burn before the cheese has had a chance to melt completely. A way around this problem is to grill at a lower heat for a longer time.

SHREDDED CHEESE

Pros: Shredded cheese melts the fastest and the most evenly.

Cons: When you're assembling a sandwich, corralling cheese shards can be a messy task. They have a tendency to fall out of the sandwich, which is bothersome. Also, pre-shredded cheeses often have anti-caking agents that prevent them from melting as smoothly as we might like.

HAND-SLICED CHEESE

Pros: These thinner slices not only melt quickly but also lie flat on your sandwich, making for easy assembly. In addition, a block of cheese usually costs less per pound than pre-sliced cheese.

Cons: It takes an extra few minutes to slice the cheese yourself (but not long at all) and you need to buy a cheese slicer (but they're not expensive).

SWEET AND TART. Apples have become a favorite panini ingredient for me—they pair well with many cheeses, as well as with pork, beef, and turkey. Depending on the flavors in the sandwich, I might choose a sweeter apple, like a Gala, or one that will bring more tartness and acidity, such as a Granny Smith. There are more than 15 recipes featuring apples in this book—check them all out!

Sweet summer peaches and nectarines are also interesting alternatives to tomatoes anytime you want to switch things up a bit.

MAKE ROOM FOR MUSHROOMS. For a substantial alternative to meat, look no further than mushrooms. These things drink up flavor like nobody's business and are quick to grill on the panini press or sauté on the stove. I use big, hearty portobello mushroom caps to make vegetarian Grilled Portobello Cheese Steak Panini (page 119), and I sauté wild mushrooms with shallots and balsamic vinegar for Turkey and Wild Mushroom Panini (page 37).

LEAFY PURSUITS. Greens such as arugula, basil, watercress, and leaf lettuce bring delicate flavor and a shot of color to panini. They do, however, have a tendency to wilt under the heat of the grill. I have three good solutions for this problem:

- Consider adding greens as a final step after grilling—open up the grilled panini and stick the greens in at the end so they'll stay nice and crisp.
- Position greens toward the middle of the sandwich, where they will be exposed to less heat.
- If all else fails, embrace wilted greens—they still taste great!

EAT YOUR VEGGIES. Whether you have leftovers on hand or you opt to grill some right on the panini press (see "Grilling Beyond Sandwiches" on page 19), vegetables make wonderful panini ingredients. I love to use grilled eggplant, asparagus, zucchini, onions, and bell peppers as well as tender raw vegetables like fennel and cabbage. You can also puree cooked legumes—beans, peas, and lentils—and spread them onto your sandwiches either in addition to or as an alternative to cheese.

WATCH THE MOISTURE. Bear in mind that the juiciness that makes many fruits and vegetables so tasty and appealing can also bog down a sandwich with too much moisture. Here are a few tips to avoid soggy bread:

- Remove the seeds from tomatoes. When possible, go for plum tomatoes (I use the Roma variety), which tend to have less pulp and seeds.
- Position wetter ingredients toward the center of your panini, away from the bread. (This goes for other wet ingredients, like sauces and coleslaw, too.)
- If you're grilling panini with juicy fruits and vegetables, consider firmer, denser, crusty breads like baguettes or ciabatta, which can stand up to moisture better than sliced bread.

CONDIMENTS

Order panini at a nice café and chances are you will be treated to a fabulous condiment inside. Basil aioli, caramelized onions, wasabi mayonnaise, honey mustard—well-placed flavorful condiments often make the difference between a so-so sandwich and one worth remembering. I often make up a big batch of Caramelized Onions (page 26) and keep them in the refrigerator to add to sandwiches and other dishes all week long. But condiments don't have to be as time-intensive as those—often it's easy enough to simply mix some herbs or garlic into store-bought mayonnaise, or spread on some fig preserves straight from the jar.

Grilling Beyond Sandwiches

Anyone who believes that a panini press is useful only for grilling sandwiches is missing out on a whole world of possibilities. We're talking about a tool with two direct heating sources—which, by the way, heat up in under five minutes. There's really no limit to what it can grill—unless, of course, the manufacturer of your grill suggests limits. Always abide by your product's manual.

MEAT, POULTRY, AND SEAFOOD

Grilling meat, poultry, and seafood on the panini press is not only a healthy way to cook but also, with the ability to grill both sides of your food at once, a much faster technique than outdoor grilling or oven roasting. Especially in the summertime, when it's often too hot to turn on the stove or stand over a hot outdoor grill, the panini press can become your best friend when it comes to getting dinner on the table. Be sure to have a drip tray in place to collect any grease that runs off (and be sure to keep this book away from the grill to avoid the side spatter!). If your press does not come equipped with a drain and/or drip tray, I don't recommend using it for grilling raw meats.

So how long will it take to cook your meat and poultry on the panini press? I'll say it again: a meat thermometer will take all the guesswork out of determining when the food is done (see page 22). Just insert the thermometer and wait until the desired temperature is reached. The United States Department of Agriculture (USDA) recommends the following safe internal cooking temperatures:

FOOD	TEMPERATURE
Beef, pork, lamb, and veal steaks, chops, and roasts	145°F (63°C)
Ground beef, pork, lamb, and veal	160°F (71°C)
Poultry	165°F (74°C)

You'll find a slew of recipes for grilled meats in this cookbook—everything from rib-eye steak (page 93) and bratwurst (page 72) to barbecued chicken thighs (page 48) and seared ahi (page 112).

FRUITS AND VEGETABLES

Whether I'm grilling zucchini or eggplant, bananas or peaches, it's all made easy with the panini press. I'll usually toss vegetables in a little olive oil, season with salt and pepper, and grill till they're tender. With fruit, often just a brush of melted butter is all that's needed to get those beautiful dark grill marks and a lightly crisp crust on the outside.

A real advantage to grilling fruits and vegetables on the panini press, as opposed to an outdoor grill, is the food won't fall through the grates. This means you can grill green beans, asparagus, and any other long, skinny, or tiny produce item you can think of, and everything will stay in place on the grill.

Tools of the Trade

In addition to a good panini press, the following tools will make preparing and grilling panini even easier.

CHEESE SLICER

As I've mentioned, slicing your own cheese is often the best way to go from a melting and ease-of-layering standpoint. A basic cheese plane or slicer isn't expensive, typically $10 to $15. You want one that is comfortable to grip, and with a metal blade that can stand up to slicing firmer cheeses without bending itself out of shape. I use the Calphalon dual-edge cheese plane.

CHEESE GRATER

Yes, slicing your own cheese is usually best, but I do grate some cheeses, especially Parmesan and other harder cheeses that take longer to melt. You can also use the grater for zesting lemons and limes as well as for finely grating garlic and onions. I prefer a box grater for these jobs. They're available at all price points, but I have to say that I have had a much easier time grating since I upgraded to a higher-end Microplane model.

SERRATED KNIFE

A sturdy serrated knife will allow you to slice through your panini cleanly without placing undue pressure on your ingredients. Even better—although it's a bit of a splurge—is an offset knife, which you'll often see used in panini cafés and restaurants. The offset design allows you to bring the knife all the way down to the cutting board without your knuckles getting in the way.

MEAT THERMOMETER

If you're going to grill meats on your panini press, I highly recommend using a meat thermometer. It's the easiest and most reliable way to ensure that meat is cooked to the desired temperature. With the OXO model I have, it's easy for me to set the temperature (it comes with preset USDA and chef recommendations), insert the probe into the meat I'm grilling, place the meat on the panini press, close the lid, and wait until the thermometer beeps to tell me that the meat is done. It eliminates all of the guesswork, and I don't lose any heat by having to open the lid repeatedly to check for doneness.

SILICONE SPATULA AND TONGS

Everything you place on the grill has to come off at some point. For this task, you'll want a silicone spatula and silicone tongs. They easily lift your food without causing any damage to the nonstick surface of the panini press.

SILICONE GRILL BRUSH

Many grills come equipped with their own grill scraper, but for those that don't, you will probably find a silicone grill brush very helpful when it comes time to clean your panini press. The soft-yet-firm bristles make it easy to scrape up the cooked-on bits that can get trapped between the grates without damaging the nonstick coating. OXO makes the excellent grill brush that I use.

SILICONE BASTING BRUSH

For brushing olive oil onto bread, vegetables, black bean patties, and more, a silicone basting or pastry brush is a useful tool. It distributes oil evenly and goes right into the dishwasher for cleanup.

POULTRY PERFECTION

Chicken, Turkey, and Duck on the Panini Press

Chicken, Brie, Fig, and Arugula Panini

▶ **Yield:** 4 panini

1 French baguette, cut into
4 portions, or
4 mini baguettes
½ cup (160 g) fig preserves
8 ounces (225 g) Brie cheese
(with or without the rind),
sliced
½ cup (10 g) baby arugula
8 ounces (225 g) carved or
deli-sliced chicken breast

For the longest time I avoided adding leafy greens to my panini out of concern that they would wilt. But after a while I really started to miss arugula, basil, cilantro, and all of the other herbs and lettuces that brought such bright, fresh flavors to my non-grilled sandwiches. Then I had a "Eureka!" moment—the closer to the middle of the sandwich I layered the greens, the less likely they were to wilt, because the middle of the sandwich is the last to receive the heat. I've been freely adding greens to panini ever since. (You might say I turned over a new leaf!)

1. Heat the panini press to medium-high heat.

2. For each sandwich: Slice off the domed top of a baguette portion to create a flat grilling surface. Split the baguette to create top and bottom halves. Spread 1 tablespoon (20 g) fig preserves inside each baguette half. Layer a few slices of Brie, a small handful of arugula, and a few slices of chicken on the bottom half of the bread. Close the sandwich with the top half.

3. Grill two panini at a time, with the lid closed, until the cheese is melted and the baguettes are toasted, 3 to 5 minutes.

Pulled BBQ Chicken Panini

▶ **Yield:** 6 panini

2½ cups (625 g) barbecue sauce

1 whole rotisserie chicken, skin and bones removed, meat shredded

6 Italian rolls, such as *filone* or ciabatta

1 cup (195 g) Caramelized Onions (recipe follows)

12 ounces (340 g) fresh mozzarella cheese, thinly sliced

Chili oil for brushing (optional)

Yes, this sandwich is messy, but I promise you won't mind. We're talking about shredded rotisserie chicken simmered in barbecue sauce, piled on Italian bread, drizzled with chili oil, and topped with fresh mozzarella and Caramelized Onions. That's worth a little untidiness, right? You can easily adjust the recipe, which was inspired by my favorite barbecued chicken pizza, to use up leftover chicken.

Look for chili oil, a spicy condiment that's been infused with chili peppers, alongside other oils or in the Asian foods section of your grocery store.

1. In a medium-size saucepan, bring the barbecue sauce to a simmer over medium heat. Add the shredded chicken and continue to simmer for another 10 minutes.

2. Heat the panini press to medium-high heat.

3. *For each sandwich:* Split a roll to create top and bottom halves. Scoop a generous amount of pulled BBQ chicken on the bottom half of the roll, followed by some Caramelized Onions and several slices of mozzarella. Close the sandwich with the top half of the roll and brush a little chili oil on the surface, if desired.

4. Grill three panini at a time, with the lid closed, until the cheese is melted and the rolls are toasted, 4 to 5 minutes.

1 tablespoon (15 ml) extra-virgin olive oil

3 medium-size onions (white, yellow, or red), halved and thinly sliced

Coarse salt and freshly ground black pepper

Caramelized Onions

▶ **Yield:** About 1 cup (195 g)

1. Heat the olive oil in a large skillet over medium heat. Add the onions and cook for 10 minutes, stirring occasionally. The onions will be soft and just barely beginning to turn brown.

2. Reduce the heat to low. Season with salt and pepper and continue to cook, stirring often to prevent scorching, until the onions are soft, deep brown, and caramelized, another 40 to 50 minutes.

Mediterranean Chicken Flatbread Panini

▶ **Yield:** 4 panini

Nothing feels homier to me than roasting a whole chicken on the weekend. Even though we're a family of four, the junior members of our household aren't quite old enough yet to hold up their end of the chicken-eating requirements necessary to finish off a whole bird in one meal. That means that we tend to have leftover chicken in the fridge at the beginning of the week, which is a blessing when you're someone who enjoys creating new kinds of sandwiches! Here, I've matched up shredded leftover chicken with some of my favorite Mediterranean flavors—hummus, olive tapenade, roasted red bell peppers, and feta—all grilled on toasty flatbread.

1. Heat the panini press to medium-high heat.

2. *For each sandwich:* Cut a pita in half across the diameter, creating two semicircles—these will become your top and bottom halves. Spread 2 tablespoons (31 g) of hummus on one pita half and 1 tablespoon (8 g) olive tapenade on the other. Top the hummus with chicken, red peppers, torn basil, and feta. Close the sandwich with the other pita, tapenade side down.

3. Grill two panini at a time, with the lid closed, until the feta is softened and the pitas are toasted, 4 to 5 minutes.

4 pita breads or other flatbreads
½ cup (123 g) hummus
4 tablespoons (34 g) olive tapenade
1 cup (140 g) shredded cooked chicken
¼ cup (45 g) sliced roasted red bell peppers
8 fresh basil leaves, roughly torn
4 ounces (115 g) crumbled feta cheese

Chicken Bacon Melt Panini

▶ **Yield:** 4 panini

2 boneless, skinless chicken breasts, halved horizontally to create 4 cutlets (about 1 pound [455 g] total)

½ teaspoon coarse salt

⅛ teaspoon freshly ground black pepper

4 tablespoons (½ stick, or 55 g) butter, at room temperature

8 slices of rustic white bread, sliced from a dense bakery loaf

½ cup (112 g) Avocado Spread (see below)

8 strips of cooked bacon

2 plum tomatoes (such as Roma), thinly sliced and seeded

4 ounces (115 g) Asiago or other sharp cheese, sliced

Once I realized just how quick and easy it was to grill chicken breasts on the panini press, it opened up a whole world of chicken sandwich options that I had never explored before. These panini are among my favorites, with simple, classic comfort-food flavors.

Use Leftovers: Swap in any leftover cooked chicken you have on hand in place of grilling chicken breasts in this recipe.

1. Heat the panini press to medium-high heat. If your panini press comes with a removable drip tray, make sure it is in place (see page 12).

2. Season both sides of the chicken breasts with salt and pepper and grill them, with the lid closed, until they're cooked to an internal temperature of 165°F (74°C), 3 to 4 minutes.

3. Unplug the grill, carefully clean the grates, and then reheat the panini press to medium-high heat.

4. *For each sandwich:* Spread butter on two slices of bread to flavor the outside of the sandwich. Flip over both slices of bread and spread 1 tablespoon (15 ml) avocado spread on the other side of each. Top one slice with 2 bacon strips, a chicken breast, tomato slices, and cheese. Close the sandwich with the other slice of bread, buttered side up.

5. Grill two panini at a time, with the lid closed, until the cheese is melted and the bread is toasted, 4 to 5 minutes.

1 medium-size ripe avocado, pitted and peeled

1 tablespoon (15 ml) freshly squeezed lemon juice

¼ teaspoon coarse salt

⅛ teaspoon cayenne pepper

Avocado Spread

▶ **Yield:** About ½ cup (112 g)

In a small food processor or blender, puree the avocado, lemon juice, salt, and cayenne until it's smooth and creamy. Give the mixture a taste and season with more salt or lemon juice as needed. This spread is best if used the day it's made.

Chicken Sausage, Apple Butter, and Fontina Panini

▶ **Yield:** 4 panini

4 fully cooked chicken-
apple sausage links
(such as Aidells)

1 ciabatta loaf, cut into
4 portions, or

4 ciabatta rolls

4 ounces (115 g) fontina
cheese, sliced

½ cup apple butter

1 cup Caramelized Onions
(page 19)

For these panini I match the intense, concentrated flavor of apple butter with equally bold smoky, nutty, and sweet flavors for a true sweet and savory mouthful.

1. Heat the panini press to medium-high heat. If your panini press comes with a removable drip tray, make sure it is in place (see page 12).

2. Slice each chicken-apple sausage link in half lengthwise without slicing all the way through, then fold open the sausage. Place the sausages, cut sides down, on the grill. Close the lid and grill the sausages until they are heated through and grill marks appear, 4 to 5 minutes.

3. *For each sandwich:* Split a ciabatta portion to create top and bottom halves. Lay cheese over the bottom half of the bread, followed by the grilled sausage and caramelized onions. Spread 2 tablespoons (28 ml) apple butter inside the top half of the bread and place it on top of the sandwich to close it.

4. Grill two panini at a time, with the lid closed, until the cheese is melted and the ciabatta is toasted, 5 to 7 minutes.

Chicken Cordon Bleu Panini

▶ **Yield:** 4 panini

It's time to take things a little retro. Chicken cordon bleu (which translates to "blue ribbon") may not have actually originated at the famed French cooking school, but it was nonetheless a winning dish for many American families in the 1960s and '70s. The key components—breaded chicken breast, cheese, and ham—transform easily into a sandwich, along with a sweet kick of honey mustard.

1. *Chicken:* Season the chicken with salt and pepper on both sides. Set up a dredging station with the flour, beaten egg, and bread crumbs each in its own separate shallow bowl. In a large skillet, heat the olive oil over medium-high heat. Dredge each piece of chicken in the flour, then the egg, then the bread crumbs, and place it carefully in the skillet. Cook the chicken for 3 to 4 minutes on each side. Transfer the chicken to a wire rack or a paper towel–lined plate to drain.

2. *Panini:* Heat the panini press to medium-high heat.

3. Whisk together the honey and Dijon mustard in a small bowl.

4. *For each sandwich:* Spread butter on two slices of bread to flavor the outside of the sandwich. Flip over both slices and spread 1 tablespoon (18 g) honey mustard on the other side of each slice. Top one slice with a breaded chicken breast, followed by ham and cheese slices. Close the sandwich with the other slice of bread, buttered side up.

5. Grill two panini at a time, with the lid closed, until the cheese is melted and the bread is toasted, 4 to 5 minutes.

CHICKEN

2 boneless, skinless chicken breasts, halved horizontally to create 4 cutlets (about 1 pound [455 g] total)
½ teaspoon coarse salt
⅛ teaspoon freshly ground black pepper
½ cup (63 g) all-purpose flour
1 large egg, beaten
½ cup (60 g) plain bread crumbs
2 tablespoons (28 ml) extra-virgin olive oil

PANINI

¼ cup (85 g) honey
¼ cup (60 g) Dijon mustard
4 tablespoons (½ stick, or 55 g) butter, at room temperature
8 slices of rustic white bread, sliced from a dense bakery loaf
4 ounces (115 g) sliced ham
4 ounces (115 g) Swiss cheese, sliced

Chicken Caesar Panini

▶ **Yield:** 4 panini

CHICKEN
4 cups (946 ml) water
¼ cup (120 g) coarse salt
2 tablespoons (40 g) honey
1 bay leaf
1 garlic clove, crushed
6 whole black peppercorns
A pinch of dried thyme
A pinch of dried parsley
1 tablespoon (15 ml) fresh-
    ly squeezed lemon juice
2 boneless, skinless
    chicken breasts,
    halved horizontally to
    create 4 cutlets (about
    1 pound [455 g] total)

PANINI
1 French baguette, cut into
    4 portions,
    or 4 mini baguettes
½ cup (120 ml) Caesar
    dressing
2 plum tomatoes (such as
    Roma), thinly sliced and
    seeded
¼ medium-size red onion,
    sliced
4 ounces (115 g) Asiago
    pressato or aged Asiago
    cheese, sliced (see Note)
4 romaine lettuce leaves

Flavorful grilled chicken breast, melty Asiago cheese, crisp romaine lettuce, tomatoes, red onions, and Caesar dressing on a toasty, crouton-like baguette—it's chicken Caesar salad's sandwich cousin. There was a café across the street from my office building in San Francisco back in my corporate days that made an excellent version, so I'd order it two or three times a week. These panini bring back some fond—if a little excessive—food memories.

1. *Chicken:* In a large bowl, stir together the water, salt, honey, bay leaf, garlic, peppercorns, thyme, parsley, and lemon juice until the salt and honey are dissolved. Add the chicken, cover the bowl with plastic wrap, and let the chicken soak in the brine for 30 to 40 minutes in the refrigerator.

2. *Panini:* Heat the panini press to medium-high heat. If your panini press comes with a removable drip tray, make sure it is in place (see page 12).

3. Remove the chicken from the brine and discard the brine. Pat the chicken cutlets dry and transfer them to the grill. Close the lid and grill the chicken until it's cooked to an internal temperature of 165°F (74°C), 3 to 4 minutes. Set the chicken aside. Unplug the grill, carefully wipe it clean, and heat it again to medium-high heat.

4. *For each sandwich:* Slice off the domed top of a baguette portion to create a flat grilling surface. Split the baguette to create top and bottom halves. Spread 1 tablespoon (15 ml) Caesar dressing inside each baguette half. Place a chicken cutlet on the bottom baguette half and top it with tomatoes, red onions, and cheese. Close the sandwich with the top baguette half.

5. Grill two panini at a time, with the lid closed, until the cheese is melted and the baguettes are toasted, 5 to 7 minutes. Open the bottom of each sandwich, fold a romaine leaf in half, and tuck it in beneath the chicken (we add the lettuce at the end so it stays fresh and crisp).

NOTE: Asiago pressato, the fresh form of Asiago cheese, melts especially well, but you can also use aged Asiago. I can find both types in the specialty cheese department at my regular grocery store.

Lemon-Thyme Chicken Panini

▶ **Yield:** 4 panini

Chicken breasts are infused with lemon zest and thyme in a quick brine, grilled in just a few minutes on the panini press and made into a panini with Feta–Goat Cheese Spread, sweet sun-dried tomatoes, and arugula. These are great panini to pack in an insulated bag to take to work or on a picnic.

1. *Chicken:* In a large bowl, stir together the water, salt, honey, bay leaf, peppercorns, thyme, lemon zest, and lemon juice until the salt and honey are dissolved. Add the chicken, cover the bowl with plastic wrap, and let the chicken soak in the brine for 30 to 40 minutes in the refrigerator.

2. *Panini:* Heat the panini press to medium-high heat. If your panini press comes with a removable drip tray, make sure it is in place (see page 12).

3. Remove the chicken from the brine and discard the brine. Pat the chicken cutlets dry and place them on the grill. Close the lid and grill the chicken until it's cooked to an internal temperature of 165°F (74°), 3 to 4 minutes.

4. *For each sandwich:* Spread butter on two slices of bread to flavor the outside of the sandwich. Flip over both slices of bread and spread a generous layer of Feta–Goat Cheese Spread on the other side of each. Top one slice with a grilled chicken cutlet, followed by a layer of arugula and sun-dried tomatoes. Close the sandwich with the other slice of bread, buttered side up.

5. Grill two panini at a time, with the lid closed, until the sandwich is heated through and the bread is toasted, 2 to 3 minutes.

Feta–Goat Cheese Spread

▶ **Yield:** About ¹/₂ cup (135 g)

In a mini food processor or in a medium-size bowl with a hand mixer, beat together the goat cheese, feta, cream, and black pepper until whipped and fluffy.

CHICKEN
4 cups (946 ml) water
¼ cup (120 g) coarse salt
2 tablespoons (40 g) honey
1 bay leaf
6 whole black peppercorns
1 teaspoon dried thyme
2 teaspoons grated lemon zest
1 tablespoon (15 ml) freshly squeezed lemon juice
2 boneless, skinless chicken breasts, halved horizontally to create 4 cutlets (about 1 pound [455 g] total)

PANINI
4 tablespoons (½ stick, or 55 g) butter, at room temperature
8 slices of rustic white bread, sliced from a dense bakery loaf
1 recipe Feta–Goat Cheese Spread (recipe follows)
1 cup (20 g) baby arugula
½ cup (55 g) sliced oil-packed sun-dried tomatoes

1 (5½-ounce, or 155 g) log goat cheese, at room temperature
1 ounce (28 g) crumbled feta cheese (about ¼ cup)
1 tablespoo (15 ml) heavy cream or half-and-half
⅛ teaspoon freshly ground black pepper

Garlic Chicken Panini

▶ **Yield:** 4 panini

CHICKEN
4 cups (946 ml) water
¼ cup (120 g) coarse salt
2 tablespoons (40 g) honey
1 bay leaf
1 garlic clove, crushed
6 whole black peppercorns
A pinch of dried thyme
A pinch of dried parsley
1 tablespoon (15 ml) freshly squeezed lemon juice
2 boneless, skinless
chicken breasts,
halved horizontally to
create 4 cutlets (about
1 pound [455 g] total)

PANINI
1 French baguette, cut into
4 portions, or
4 mini baguettes
1 recipe Basil-Garlic
Mayonnaise (recipe
follows)
½ cup (150 g) sliced
marinated artichoke
hearts
½ cup (90 g) sliced roasted
red bell peppers
4 ounces (115 g) Swiss
cheese, sliced

When I was a little kid growing up in the Silicon Valley, my family always managed to unwittingly choose the weekend of the annual garlic festival to drive south through the city of Gilroy—the "Garlic Capital of the World." The not-so-subtle signals would reach our nostrils miles before we reached the city limits. I didn't really know what garlic was, but I was a little afraid of it!

These days, garlic and I have a much friendlier relationship—it's one of my favorite big-flavor ingredients, and I cook with it nearly every day. But rest assured, the garlic flavor in these panini comes from the basil-garlic mayonnaise, and it isn't overwhelming. You can still kiss your loved ones after eating these sandwiches . . . which is a good thing, because someone will definitely want to kiss you if you make one for them.

1. *Chicken:* In a large bowl, stir together the water, salt, honey, bay leaf, garlic, peppercorns, thyme, parsley, and lemon juice until the salt and honey are dissolved. Add the chicken, cover the bowl with plastic wrap, and let the chicken soak in the brine for 30 to 40 minutes in the refrigerator.

2. *Panini:* Heat the panini press to medium-high heat. If your panini press comes with a removable drip tray, make sure it is in place (see page 12).

3. Remove the chicken from the brine and discard the brine. Pat the chicken cutlets dry and transfer them to the grill. Close the lid and grill the chicken until it's cooked to an internal temperature of 165°F (74°C), 3 to 4 minutes. Set the chicken aside. Unplug the grill, carefully wipe it clean, and heat it again to medium-high heat.

4. *For each sandwich:* Slice off the domed top of a baguette portion to create a flat grilling surface. Split the baguette to create top and bottom halves. Spread 1 tablespoon (14 g) of Basil-Garlic Mayonnaise inside each baguette half. Place a chicken cutlet on the bottom baguette half and top it with artichoke hearts, roasted red peppers, and cheese. Close the sandwich with the top baguette half.

5. Grill two panini at a time, with the lid closed, until the cheese is melted and the baguettes are toasted, 5 to 7 minutes.

Basil-Garlic Mayonnaise

▶ **Yield:** About ½ cup (115 g)

This big-flavor condiment not only dresses up any chicken or turkey sandwich, it's also fabulous on burgers or as a dip for veggies or French fries.

½ cup (20 g) coarsely chopped fresh basil
1 garlic clove, smashed
⅛ teaspoon coarse salt
A dash of cayenne pepper
½ cup (115 g) mayonnaise

Blend the basil, garlic, salt, and cayenne in a food processor until well combined. Add the mayonnaise and continue to blend until smooth. Transfer the mayonnaise to a small bowl, cover, and refrigerate for 30 minutes to allow the flavors to meld.

Red, White, and Blue Cheese Panini

▶ **Yield:** 4 panini

1 tablespoon (15 ml) extra-virgin olive oil

8 slices rosemary olive-oil bread or sourdough bread, sliced from a dense bakery loaf

4 tablespoons (160 g) mayonnaise

8 ounces (225 g) carved or deli-sliced roast turkey

8 strips of cooked bacon

1 medium-size ripe avocado, pitted, peeled, and thinly sliced

8 oil-packed sun-dried tomatoes, thinly sliced

4 ounces (115 g) crumbled Gorgonzola cheese

8 romaine lettuce leaves

When I'm at the hair salon, the conversation with my super-hip British stylist quite often turns to food. Sometime around the blow-dry and flat-iron stage I usually extract one or two excellent recommendations for places to eat in downtown San Diego. He introduced me to a lovely bakery café called Con Pane and one of their signature sandwiches, the Turkey Cobb. Roasted turkey, bacon, avocado, sweet roasted Roma tomatoes, just a sprinkling of Gorgonzola cheese, and romaine lettuce on their airy, house-baked rosemary olive-oil bread—Con Pane has created an absolute masterpiece with this one. For my grilled version, I wait until the sandwich comes off the grill to add the romaine. That way I can have the toasted bread and soft Gorgonzola while still keeping the greens fresh and crisp.

On my blog I called these my Red, White, and Blue Cheese Panini in honor of the Fourth of July, but I'll eagerly devour this sandwich any day of the year.

1. Heat the panini press to medium-high heat.

2. *For each sandwich:* Brush a little olive oil on two slices of bread to flavor the outside of the sandwich. Flip over one slice and spread 1 tablespoon (14 g) mayonnaise on the other side. Top the mayonnaise with turkey, bacon, avocado, tomatoes, and Gorgonzola cheese. Close the sandwich with the other slice of bread, oiled side up.

3. Grill two panini at a time, with the lid closed, until the cheese has softened and the bread is toasted, 3 to 4 minutes.

4. Remove each sandwich from the grill, flip it over, and carefully remove the bottom slice of bread. Add 2 lettuce leaves and replace the bottom slice of bread.

Turkey and Wild Mushroom Panini

▶ **Yield:** 4 panini

My husband was away at a conference in Las Vegas when I emailed him about these panini. I couldn't wait to tell him that I'd come up with a turkey and *mushroom* sandwich that I loved. Me, the one who is more commonly known to *remove* mushrooms from dishes. This combination is fabulous!

1. Heat the panini press to medium-high heat.

2. *For each sandwich:* Split a ciabatta portion to create top and bottom halves. Spoon a generous layer of Sautéed Wild Mushrooms inside the bottom half, followed by a handful of watercress and a few slices of turkey and cheese. Spread Dijon mustard inside the top half and place it on top of the sandwich to close it.

3. Grill two panini at a time, with the lid closed, until the cheese is melted and the ciabatta is toasted, 4 to 5 minutes.

1 ciabatta loaf, cut into 4 portions, or 4 ciabatta rolls
1 recipe Sautéed Wild Mushrooms (recipe follows)
4 ounces (115 g) watercress
8 ounces (225 g) carved or deli-sliced roast turkey
4 ounces (115 g) Swiss cheese, sliced
3 tablespoons (45 g) Dijon mustard

Sautéed Wild Mushrooms

▶ **Yield:** About 1¼ cups (165 g)

In my experience, there aren't many foods that can't be remarkably enhanced by sautéing them in olive oil and butter with garlic and shallots and finishing them with some balsamic vinegar. Mushrooms, it turns out, are no exception.

Heat the olive oil and butter in a large skillet over medium heat until the butter is melted. Add the shallots and garlic and cook, stirring frequently, until they're fragrant, 1 to 2 minutes. Add the mushrooms and cook, stirring occasionally, until the mushrooms are tender, 5 to 7 minutes. Stir in the balsamic vinegar and parsley and season with salt and pepper to taste.

1 tablespoon (15 ml) extra-virgin olive oil
1 tablespoon (14 g) unsalted butter
¼ cup (40 g) thinly sliced shallots
2 garlic cloves, minced
2½ cups (175 g) sliced wild mushrooms, such as shiitake (stemmed), chanterelle, or porcini
2 teaspoons balsamic vinegar
1 tablespoon (4 g) chopped fresh parsley
Coarse salt and freshly ground black pepper

Turkey, Cranberry, and Brie Panini

▶ **Yield:** 4 panini

1 multigrain baguette, cut into 4 portions, or 4 mini baguettes

4 ounces (115 g) Brie cheese (with or without the rind), sliced

8 ounces (225 g) carved or deli-sliced roast turkey

4 tablespoons (70 g) whole-berry cranberry sauce

Those who truly love the combination of roast turkey and cranberry sauce eat it all year long, not just at Thanksgiving. But the great thing about Thanksgiving is that it brings you an ample supply of carved turkey and, quite often, lots of leftover cranberry sauce as well. Just pick up some Brie and a baguette or two while you're shopping for the big feast and you'll be able to parlay your leftovers into these delectable panini for days.

1. Heat the panini press to medium-high heat.

2. *For each sandwich:* Slice off the domed top of a baguette portion to create a flat grilling surface. Split the baguette to create top and bottom halves. Layer Brie and turkey on the bottom half of the baguette. Spread 1 tablespoon (16 g) of cranberry sauce inside the top baguette half and place it on top of the sandwich to close it.

3. Grill two panini at a time, with the lid closed, until the cheese is melted and the baguettes are toasted, 5 to 7 minutes.

Turkey, Fig, Gorgonzola, and Arugula Panini

▶ **Yield:** 4 panini

4 tablespoons (½ stick, or 55 g) butter, at room temperature

8 slices of whole-grain bread, sliced from a dense bakery loaf

½ cup (160 g) fig preserves

8 ounces (225 g) carved or deli-sliced roast turkey

1 cup (20 g) baby arugula

2 ounces (55 g) crumbled Gorgonzola or other blue cheese

I'm firmly in the "love it" camp when it comes to Gorgonzola, especially when it's balanced with something sweet, like fig preserves. The whole-grain bread for these panini brings a nuttiness that also pairs perfectly with a strong-flavored cheese like Gorgonzola. Add some turkey and peppery arugula, and you've got a winning sandwich.

1. Heat the panini press to medium-high heat.

2. *For each sandwich:* Spread butter on two slices of bread to flavor the outside of the sandwich. Flip over both slices and spread a generous layer of fig preserves on the other side of each. On one slice of bread layer turkey, a small handful of arugula, and a sprinkling of Gorgonzola. Close the sandwich with the other slice of bread, buttered side up.

3. Grill two panini at a time, with the lid closed, until the cheese is softened and the bread is toasted, 4 to 5 minutes.

Turkey Rachel Panini

▶ **Yield:** 4 panini

If you know the traditional Reuben (page 86), you're familiar with a robust sandwich piled with corned beef or pastrami, sauerkraut, Swiss cheese, and Russian dressing, served on rye bread. A turkey Reuben, also known as a Rachel or a California Reuben, substitutes turkey and coleslaw for the beef and sauerkraut. To bring in extra Thanksgiving flavor—because I seem to make most of my turkey sandwiches around Thanksgiving—I make a cranberry Russian dressing and toss it with cabbage for a very zesty—and pink—coleslaw.

4 tablespoons (½ stick, or 55 g) butter, at room temperature
8 slices of rye bread, sliced from a dense bakery loaf
4 ounces (115 g) Swiss cheese, sliced
8 ounces (225 g) carved or deli-sliced roast turkey
¾ cup (150 g) Cranberry Coleslaw (recipe follows)

1. Heat the panini press to medium-high heat.

2. *For each sandwich:* Spread butter on two slices of bread to flavor the outside of the sandwich. Flip over one slice and top the other side with cheese, turkey, a few spoonfuls of Cranberry Coleslaw, and then more turkey and more cheese. Close the sandwich with the other slice of bread, buttered side up.

3. Grill two panini at a time, with the lid closed, until the cheese is melted and the bread is toasted, 4 to 5 minutes.

Cranberry Coleslaw

▶ **Yield:** About 2 cups (400 g)

This tangy-sweet slaw, with a kick of horseradish, is just as tasty as a stand-alone side dish as it is layered on your leftover Thanksgiving turkey panini.

⅓ cup (75 g) mayonnaise
2 tablespoons (35 g) whole-berry cranberry sauce
2 teaspoons freshly grated horseradish
1 teaspoon Worcestershire sauce
Coarse salt and freshly ground black pepper, to taste
2 cups (140 g) shredded green cabbage or packaged coleslaw mix

1. Whisk together the mayonnaise, cranberry sauce, horseradish, and Worcestershire sauce in a small bowl. Season the dressing with salt and pepper to taste.

2. In a medium-size bowl, toss the cabbage with the dressing.

Turkey-Apple Panini with Fig and Gruyère

▶ **Yield:** 4 panini

4 tablespoons (½ stick, or 55 g) butter, at room temperature

8 slices of rustic whole-grain bread, sliced from a dense bakery loaf

½ cup (160 g) fig preserves

8 ounces (225 g) carved or deli-sliced roast turkey

1 Granny Smith apple, cored and thinly sliced

8 ounces (225 g) Gruyère cheese, thinly sliced

Sandwiches like these taste like autumn to me. It's when figs and apples are at their peak and thoughts of golden roast turkey begin to float through my mind in anticipation of Thanksgiving. They're a sweet and savory hallmark of one of the coziest times of the year.

1. Heat the panini press to medium-high heat.

2. *For each sandwich:* Spread butter on two slices of bread to flavor the outside of the sandwich. Flip over both slices and spread 1 tablespoon (20 g) fig preserves on the other side of each. Top one slice with turkey, apples, and cheese. Close the sandwich with the other slice of bread, buttered side up.

3. Grill two panini at a time, with the lid closed, until the cheese is melted and the bread is toasted, 4 to 5 minutes.

Smoked Turkey Croque Monsieur Panini

▶ **Yield:** 4 panini

The name "croque monsieur" is based on the French verb *croquer*, which means "to crunch." While a traditional croque monsieur is blanketed with a rich, cheesy Mornay sauce, with my grilled version of this classic sandwich, you get to bite through a tangy Parmesan crust, a nod to its crunchy origins.

1. In a small bowl, mix the butter and Parmesan cheese until they are well combined.

2. Heat the panini press to medium-high heat.

3. *For each sandwich:* Spread Parmesan butter on two slices of bread. Flip over both slices and spread Dijon mustard on the other side of each. Top one slice with Gruyère cheese, turkey, and more cheese. Close the sandwich with the other slice of bread, buttered, side up.

4. Grill two panini at a time, with the lid closed, until the cheese is melted and the bread is toasted with a crispy crust, 4 to 5 minutes.

- 4 tablespoons (½ stick, or 55 g) butter, at room temperature
- 1 ounce (28 g) shredded Parmesan cheese (about ¼ cup)
- 8 slices of rustic white bread, sliced from a dense bakery loaf
- 4 tablespoons (60 g) Dijon mustard
- 8 ounces (225 g) Gruyère cheese, sliced
- 8 ounces (225 g) sliced smoked turkey breast

Duck Breast Club Panini

▶ **Yield:** 4 panini

4 tablespoons (½ stick, or 55 g) butter, at room temperature (optional)

8 slices of sourdough bread, sliced from a dense bakery loaf

2 tablespoons (28 g) mayonnaise

8 strips of cooked bacon

2 Grilled Duck Breasts (page 47), sliced across the grain

½ cup (10 g) baby arugula

2 plum tomatoes (such as Roma), thinly sliced and seeded

4 ounces (115 g) Brie cheese (with or without the rind), sliced

My husband came up with the concept for duck club panini—slices of succulent duck breast layered with strips of smoky bacon, fresh tomatoes and arugula, and creamy Brie. It's a decadent combination for sure, but I doubt you'll have any trouble finding someone willing to split one of these with you.

If you're making the panini right after grilling the duck breasts, it's up to you whether to scrape down the grill. I like the extra-crispy crunch the residual duck fat adds to the panini, so in this case, I hold off on cleaning until the end.

1. Heat the panini press to medium-high heat.

2. *For each sandwich:* Spread butter on two slices of bread to flavor the outside of the sandwich (you may want to skip this step if you are taking advantage of the residual duck fat on the grill). Flip over one slice of bread and spread a little mayonnaise on the other side. Top the mayonnaise with 2 bacon strips, some duck slices, a small handful of arugula, tomato slices, and Brie. Close the sandwich with the other slice of bread, buttered side up (if you're using butter).

3. Grill two panini at a time, with the lid closed, until the cheese is melted and the bread is toasted, 4 to 5 minutes.

No-Fuss, No-Flip Chicken Quesadillas

▶ **Yield:** 4 quesadillas

I'll tell you one thing that really impresses me: when chefs can easily and expertly flip food in a skillet with just a quick flick of the wrist. I watch in complete awe—this is not a skill I currently possess. I can usually flip pancakes if the batter is thick enough, but a quesadilla full of shredded cheese and other loose toppings? Forget it.

Enter the panini press, with its ability to cook from both the top and bottom at the same time. It's by far the easiest way that I know of to cook quesadillas and other dishes that you'd otherwise have to flip.

1 tablespoon (15 ml) vegetable oil
8 flour tortillas (8 inches, or 20 cm each)
8 ounces (225 g) shredded cheese, such as cheddar, Monterey Jack, or Colby, or a mixture (about 2 cups)
1 can (4 ounces, or 115 g) of diced green chiles, drained
1 cup (140 g) shredded cooked chicken
Salsa, for serving

1. Heat the panini press to medium-high heat.

2. *For each quesadilla:* Brush a little oil on two tortillas. Flip over one tortilla and scatter on a few tablespoons (21 to 28 g) of cheese, leaving a 1-inch (1.3 cm) margin around the edge to avoid too much ooze during melting. Top the cheese with a few tablespoons (24 to 32 g) of green chiles, some shredded chicken, and more cheese. Place the other tortilla, oiled side up, on top.

3. Carefully transfer one quesadilla to the grill and close the lid. Grill the quesadilla until the cheese is melted and the tortilla is crisped, 3 to 4 minutes. Repeat with the rest of the tortillas.

4. Cut the quesadillas into wedges and serve with salsa.

Spatchcocked Game Hen

▶ **Yield:** 2 servings

1 Cornish game hen (1½ to 2 pounds [680 to 900 g])
1 tablespoon (15 ml) extra-virgin olive oil
½ teaspoon coarse salt
¼ teaspoon freshly ground black pepper

"Spatchcock" is a funny word, but it basically just means to butterfly. Removing the backbone of a chicken—or, in this case, a small game hen to fit on the panini press—and opening it up flat allows the bird to cook quickly and evenly. On a panini press, with heat from both sides, you can grill a game hen in under 20 minutes—about half the time it would take to roast it.

Game hens are often sold frozen, so be sure to allow plenty of time for yours to defrost in the refrigerator (it may take more than a day). This recipe is a very simple preparation, but you should always feel free to experiment with your favorite seasonings and spice rubs.

1. Heat the panini press to medium-high heat. If your panini press comes with a removable drip tray, make sure it is in place (see page 12).

2. Lay the game hen, breast side down, on a cutting board. With sturdy kitchen shears, cut through the ribs along both sides of the backbone, from tail to neck, to remove it (discard the backbone or save it to make chicken stock).

3. Open the hen out flat, still breast side down. Using a small paring knife, make a slice down the middle of the keel bone (the diamond-shaped white bone between the two breasts). Next, carefully cut around the thin, oblong strip of cartilage that runs down the middle of the hen. Once you've separated the cartilage from the flesh, reach in with your hands and lift it out and discard it. Don't worry if you're not able to do this as cleanly as you'd like—no one will notice.

4. Pat the hen dry and rub olive oil all over the bird. Season the hen on all sides with salt and pepper.

5. Carefully transfer the hen to the grill, skin side up, and close the lid. Grill the hen until it is cooked to an internal temperature of 165°F (74°), 18 to 20 minutes.

Grilled Duck Breasts

▶ **Yield:** 4 servings

I grilled duck breast after duck breast on my panini press, trying to figure out how to achieve that irresistible crispy skin everyone loves. Over and over again I got the same result— quickly cooked meat with a rubbery fat cap on top. With one duck breast left, and I went for a Hail Mary pass—cooking the duck, skin side down, *with the grill open.* After about 9 minutes, I peered under the duck to find what had been eluding me thus far: browned, crispy skin! I flipped the duck breast and closed the lid, and the other side finished cooking several minutes later. This, friends, was a triumphant moment in panini grilling.

Note: If your panini press doesn't allow you to adjust the temperature, I wouldn't recommend using it to grill duck breasts. To render the duck's fat slowly, it's important to be able to cook it over lower heat—the default heat setting on a panini press without temperature adjustment may be too high to achieve this.

2 boneless, skin-on duck breasts (about 12 ounces [340 g])
Coarse salt and freshly ground black pepper

1. Heat the panini press to medium-low heat. If your panini press comes with a removable drip tray, make sure it is in place (see page 12).

2. Pat the duck breasts dry with a paper towel. With a sharp knife, score the fat layer on the duck breasts by carefully slicing through the skin just until you hit the meat (don't slice through the meat). Make several slices, about an inch (2.5 cm) apart, in a crosshatch pattern.

3. Season the duck generously on both sides with salt and pepper.

4. Open the panini press lid and lay one or both duck breasts on the grill (work in batches if only one will fit), skin side down. Leaving the lid open, grill the duck until much of the fat has rendered and the skin is brown and crispy, 9 to 11 minutes. Since grill temperatures vary, it may take more or less time for the duck to render its fat, crisp up, and brown on your grill. Using tongs, flip the breast(s) over and close the lid. Grill until the meat is cooked to an internal temperature of 150°F (66°), another 3 to 4 minutes. Transfer the duck to a cutting board and allow it to rest for 10 minutes before slicing it across the grain.

Citrus-Marinated Grilled Chicken

▶ **Yield:** 2 servings

¼ cup (60 ml) extra-virgin olive oil

Juice of 1 orange (about ¼ cup [60 ml])

Juice of 1 lime (about 2 tablespoons [28 ml])

Juice of 1 lemon (about 2 tablespoons [28 ml])

¼ cup (4 g) chopped fresh cilantro

2 garlic cloves, minced

1 serrano chile, seeded and minced

¼ teaspoon ground cumin

2 whole bone-in, skin-on chicken legs (drumstick and thigh), or 4 bone-in, skin-on chicken thighs (about 1½ pounds [680 g])

½ teaspoon coarse salt

¼ teaspoon freshly ground black pepper

Corn or flour tortillas, for serving

Chopped tomatoes, for serving

Chopped red onion, for serving

Fresh cilantro leaves, for serving

If you've ever wondered what makes the *pollo asado*, or grilled chicken, at Mexican restaurants so succulent and mouthwatering, the secret is often a citrus marinade. Lemons, limes, oranges—a good soak in their acidic juices makes chicken incredibly tender and flavorful. Serve it with warm tortillas, tomatoes, red onions, and cilantro. Consider grilling up a second batch—there should be enough remaining marinade—and then shred the chicken for No-Fuss, No-Flip Chicken Quesadillas (page 45).

1. Combine the oil, citrus juices, cilantro, garlic, chile, and cumin in a large zipper-top plastic bag. Add the chicken, seal the bag, and roll the chicken around a bit in the marinade to coat it well. Marinate the chicken in the refrigerator for 2 to 4 hours.

2. Heat the panini press to medium-high heat. If your panini press comes with a removable drip tray, make sure it is in place (see page 12).

3. Remove the chicken from the marinade, discarding the leftover marinade. Blot the excess liquid from the meat with paper towels and season both sides of the chicken with salt and pepper. Place the chicken on the grill, positioning it toward the center of the grill to ensure that the heat reaches all sides. Grill the chicken, with the lid closed, until it's cooked to an internal temperature of 165°F (74°C), 18 to 20 minutes.

4. Serve with warm tortillas and bowls of chopped tomatoes, chopped red onions, and cilantro for tacos.

HIGH ON THE HOG

Pork on the Panini Press

Spicy Elvis Panini

▶ **Yield:** 4 panini

Peanut butter, bananas, and bacon—really? I avoided trying the famous Elvis sandwich for the longest time. It may have been a favorite of the King of Rock 'n' Roll, but that combination just didn't scream "Love Me Tender" to me. That is, until the day my friend Amanda introduced me to a new twist on peanut butter: spicy. She had mixed sriracha—a Thai hot pepper sauce—into peanut butter and slathered it on bread and could not contain her excitement over her culinary discovery. Suddenly, I began to look at peanut butter with new eyes and new possibilities— possibilities that could allow the inclusion of bananas and bacon.

Oh all right, I loved it. And I think you will, too, especially if you go for ripe, sweet bananas—perfectly yellow with a little bite to them, not mushy. It's completely up to you just how spicy to make things, but that little kick of heat in combination with the sweet, salty, and smoky flavors in this sandwich is definitely enough to get your taste buds "All Shook Up."

½ cup (130 g) creamy or chunky peanut butter

½ to 1 teaspoon sriracha or other hot pepper sauce

4 tablespoons (½ stick, or 55 g) butter, at room temperature

8 slices of rustic white bread, sliced from a dense bakery loaf

2 ripe bananas, thinly sliced

8 strips of cooked bacon

1. Heat the panini press to medium-high heat.

2. Mix the peanut butter and sriracha in a small bowl until well combined.

3. *For each sandwich:* Spread butter on two slices of bread to flavor the outside of the sandwich. Flip over both slices and spread 1 tablespoon (16 g) spicy peanut butter on each. Top one slice of bread with sliced bananas and 2 bacon strips. Close the sandwich with the other slice of bread, buttered side up.

4. Grill two panini at a time, with the lid closed, until the ingredients are warmed through and the bread is toasted, 2 to 3 minutes.

Ham, Apple, and Smoked Cheddar Panini with a Brown Sugar Crust

▶ **Yield:** 4 panini

4 tablespoons (½ stick, or 55 g) butter, at room temperature

8 slices of rustic multigrain bread, sliced from a dense bakery loaf

4 ounces (115 g) smoked cheddar cheese, sliced

8 ounces (225 g) sliced ham

1 sweet apple, such as Gala or Jonagold, cored and thinly sliced

2 tablespoons (30 g) packed brown sugar

Pretty please, with sugar on top? The plea is just as convincing to me now as an adult as it was when I was seven years old, begging my mom to let me ride my banana-seat bike around the cul-de-sac. And let me tell you, brown sugar sprinkled on a ham and cheese sandwich tastes really amazing. The bread gets a sweet crust on the outside just like on a baked ham. Matched with the smoked cheddar cheese and the salty ham, the combination is positively palate-pleasing.

I first got the sugar-crusting idea from the brown sugar–crusted raspberry and mozzarella panini that Giada De Laurentiis makes. While I can't in good health conscience recommend that you put sugar crusts on your panini all the time, definitely keep this sweet little secret in your back pocket for an occasional treat.

1. Heat the panini press to medium-high heat.

2. *For each sandwich:* Spread butter on two slices of bread to flavor the outside of the sandwich. Flip over one slice and layer on cheese, ham, apple slices, and more cheese. Close the sandwich with the other slice of bread, buttered side up. Sprinkle some brown sugar on top.

3. Grill two panini at a time, with the lid closed, until the cheese is melted and the bread is toasted, with a brown sugar crust, 4 to 5 minutes.

Ham, Brie, and Apple Butter–Mustard Panini

▶ **Yield:** 4 panini

A few slices of salty ham, creamy melted Brie, and some spicy Dijon mustard on a baguette—it doesn't get much better than this simple, classic French sandwich combination. Well, unless maybe you add a little apple butter to the mix.

Apple butter may not be the first condiment you think of when it comes to panini, but perhaps it should be. Apples pair supremely well with cheese. In spread form, you can use it on its own or mix it with another spread—such as Dijon mustard—to add sweet, fruity notes to a sandwich. Especially in autumn, when apples are at their peak, a seasonal touch like this will make your sandwiches extra special.

1. Heat the panini press to medium-high heat.

2. In a small bowl, whisk together the apple butter and Dijon mustard.

3. *For each sandwich:* Slice off the domed top of a baguette portion to create a flat grilling surface. Split the baguette to create top and bottom halves. Spread the apple butter–mustard mixture inside each baguette half. Layer ham and Brie on the bottom half. Close the sandwich with the top half.

4. Grill two panini at a time, with the lid closed, until the cheese is melted and the baguettes are toasted, 4 to 5 minutes.

3 tablespoons (51 g) apple butter
1 tablespoon (15 g) Dijon mustard
1 seeded baguette, cut into 4 portions, or 4 mini baguettes
8 ounces (225 g) sliced ham
4 ounces (115 g) Brie cheese (with or without the rind), sliced

Serrano Ham, Manchego, and Membrillo Panini

▶ **Yield:** 4 panini

1 French baguette, cut into 4 portions, or 4 mini baguettes

4 tablespoons (80 g) membrillo (quince paste; see Note)

4 ounces (115 g) Manchego cheese, sliced

8 ounces (225 g) sliced Serrano ham

These panini require a few special Spanish ingredients, but I promise it's worth the effort to seek them out. Serrano ham (*jamón serrano*) is similar to prosciutto, but it's cured for a longer time to produce even deeper flavor and a firmer texture. I nearly swore off all other hams the first time I tasted it. Membrillo is a sweet, firm quince paste that's most commonly paired with Manchego, my favorite sheep's milk cheese. Grill them all together on a crusty baguette and you've got wonderfully flavorful, if a bit pricey, Spanish-style panini.

1. Heat the panini press to medium-high heat.

2. *For each sandwich:* Slice off the domed top of a baguette portion to create a flat grilling surface. Split the baguette to create top and bottom halves. Spread 1 tablespoon (20 g) membrillo inside the bottom half of the baguette. Top the membrillo with cheese, ham, and more cheese. Close the sandwich with the top baguette half.

3. Grill two panini at a time, with the lid closed, until the cheese is melted and the baguettes are toasted, 7 to 9 minutes.

NOTE: Look for membrillo, Manchego, and Serrano ham at Whole Foods Market or other specialty grocers or at Hispanic markets. You can also find membrillo at gourmet retailers such as Dean & DeLuca.

Soppressata Panini with Mozzarella and Pesto

▶ **Yield:** 4 panini

When I wrote about these panini on the blog, I described them as "The Best Sandwiches I Never Had." That's because the first time I encountered them, at Armandino Batali's renowned Salumi restaurant in Seattle, I was five months pregnant and cured meats were off the table for me, so to speak. While I made do with a rice salad (comforted by the fact that Mr. Batali was having the same at a small table across from us), I longingly observed my husband savor his garlicky, house-made soppressata sandwich.

My grilled version of that fabulous sandwich can best be described as "pizza-like." The flavor of the soppressata reminds me a lot of pepperoni. There are only a few simple ingredients in this sandwich, but they combine to create something extraordinarily tasty.

1 ciabatta loaf, cut into 4 portions, or 4 ciabatta rolls
½ cup (130 g) basil pesto
8 ounces (225 g) fresh mozzarella cheese, sliced
4 ounces (115 g) sliced sweet soppressata or Genoa salami

1. Heat the panini press to medium-high heat.

2. *For each sandwich:* Split a ciabatta portion to create top and bottom halves. Spread some pesto inside each bread half. On the bottom half, layer on cheese and soppressata. Close the sandwich with the top ciabatta half.

3. Grill two panini at a time, with the lid closed, until the cheese is melted and the ciabatta is toasted, 5 to 7 minutes.

Grilled Asparagus Panini with Prosciutto and Mozzarella

▶ **Yield:** 4 panini

8 ounces (225 g) asparagus, trimmed to the length of a focaccia portion

2 teaspoons (??g) extra-virgin olive oil

Coarse salt and freshly ground black pepper

1 focaccia, cut into 4 portions

4 ounces (115 g) sliced prosciutto

8 ounces (225 g) fresh mozzarella cheese, sliced

Since asparagus and prosciutto make such a wonderful flavor duo, I created this panini recipe, adding some fresh mozzarella for that stretchy cheese effect—and to keep the asparagus in place. Keep this recipe in mind for springtime, when fresh asparagus is at its peak.

1. Heat the panini press to medium-high heat.

2. In a large bowl, toss the asparagus in the olive oil and season it with salt and pepper to taste. Grill the asparagus, with the lid closed, until they're cooked through and grill marks appear, 3 to 4 minutes. Set them aside.

3. Unplug the grill and carefully clean the grates. Reheat the grill to medium-high heat.

4. *For each sandwich:* Split a focaccia portion to create top and bottom halves. Place some prosciutto inside the bottom half. Top it with cheese and as many grilled asparagus spears as will fit securely. Close the sandwich with the other focaccia half.

5. Grill two panini at a time, with the lid closed, until the cheese is melted and the focaccia is toasted, 4 to 5 minutes.

Fig, Smoked Gouda, and Prosciutto Panini Stackers

▶ **Yield:** 12 stackers

The burger world has "sliders;" I like to think of mini panini as "stackers." You can stack up these little sandwiches alongside a cup of piping-hot soup for lunch or pass them on a tray as appetizers. I first came up with this sweet and smoky fig, Gouda, and prosciutto combo to accompany velvety butternut squash soup, but it would be a wonderful complement to all sorts of savory chowders or bisques as well.

1. Heat the panini press to medium-high heat.

2. Cut the prosciutto and smoked Gouda in half to fit onto the baguette slices.

3. Top half of the baguette slices with a thin layer of fig preserves, a piece of prosciutto, and a piece of smoked Gouda. Close all of the sandwiches with the remaining baguette slices.

4. In batches, grill the panini, with the lid closed, until the cheese is melted and the baguettes are toasted, 4 to 5 minutes.

24 French baguette slices, ¼ inch (6 mm) thick
6 slices (about 3 ounces, or 85 g) prosciutto
6 slices (about 6 ounces, or 170 g) smoked Gouda cheese
¼ cup (80 g) fig preserves

Antipasto Panini

▶ **Yield:** 4 panini

1 ciabatta loaf, cut into 4
portions, or
4 ciabatta rolls

4 tablespoons olive (325 g)
tapenade

8 ounces (225 g) fresh
mozzarella cheese, sliced

4 ounces (115 g) thinly
sliced prosciutto

8 ounces (225 g) sliced
hot soppressata or other
salami

¼ cup (45 g) sliced roasted
red bell peppers

½ cup (150 g) sliced marinated artichoke hearts

If I'm making sandwiches for friends and I'm not sure what kinds of flavors they'll like, I'll either go for a really basic grilled cheese or all the way to the other end of the spectrum with a big-flavored bonanza, such as these panini. They're some of my favorites—basically an antipasto platter on a sandwich, with Italian cured meats, mozzarella, roasted peppers, marinated artichokes, and olive tapenade. Not only are they fabulous on the grill, but these panini also make great cold sandwiches—just assemble them, wrap them up, and bring them to your next picnic!

1. Heat the panini press to medium-high heat.

2. *For each sandwich:* Split a ciabatta portion to create top and bottom halves. Spread a little olive tapenade inside both halves. On the bottom half, layer a few slices of mozzarella, prosciutto, hot soppressata, roasted red peppers, and artichoke hearts. Close the sandwich with the top ciabatta half.

3. Grill two panini at a time, with the lid closed, until the cheese is melted and the ciabatta is toasted, 4 to 5 minutes.

Salami, Prosciutto, and Provolone Panini

▶ **Yield:** *4 panini*

This is my grilled version of a fantastic Italian Combo cold sandwich I ordered at a shop called (appropriately) Panino in the tony little town of Montecito, California, just next door to Santa Barbara. I contemplated naming this sandwich the "Don Johnson" because I spotted the *Miami Vice* actor while I was there! What makes these panini stand out is the Italian-style salsa that coats the inside of the ciabatta, adding tons of fresh, zesty flavor.

1. *Salsa:* Combine the tomatoes, cucumbers, bell peppers, red onion, basil, capers, olive oil, and vinegar in a small glass bowl. Season the salsa with salt and pepper to taste. Cover the bowl and let it sit for 1 hour at room temperature to let the flavors meld.

2. *Panini:* Heat the panini press to medium-high heat.

3. *For each sandwich:* Split a ciabatta portion to create top and bottom halves. Spoon some salsa inside the bottom half. Add cheese, salami, prosciutto, more cheese, and more Salsa. Close the sandwich with the top ciabatta half.

4. Grill two panini at a time, with the lid closed, until the cheese is melted and the ciabatta is toasted, 5 to 7 minutes.

SALSA
- ½ cup (90 g) chopped seeded plum tomatoes
- ¼ cup (35 g) chopped seeded cucumber
- ¼ cup (38 g) chopped green bell pepper
- ¼ cup (40 g) chopped red onion
- 2 tablespoons (28 ml) chopped fresh basil
- 1 tablespoon (17 g) capers, rinsed and chopped
- 2 tablespoons (28 ml) extra-virgin olive oil
- 2 tablespoons (28 ml) red wine vinegar
- Coarse salt and freshly ground black pepper

PANINI
- 1 ciabatta loaf, cut into 4 portions, or 4 ciabatta rolls
- 4 ounces (115 g) provolone cheese, sliced
- 4 ounces (115 g) Genoa salami, sliced
- 4 ounces (115 g) thinly sliced prosciutto

Pepperoni Pizza Panini

▶ **Yield:** 4 panini

4 flatbreads, such as naan
  or pita
½ cup (125 g) marinara
  sauce
8 ounces (225 g) fresh
  mozzarella cheese, sliced
4 ounces (115 g) sliced
  pepperoni
8 fresh basil leaves, torn

Of all the panini ideas that people have suggested to me—it tends to be a popular topic of conversation—Pepperoni Pizza Panini is probably the most common. I'm not quite sure why that is. I'm guessing it's because it was a rather obvious omission from my blog for the longest time. Honestly, I didn't think it was worth posting a recipe for something that everyone in America knows how to make—pepperoni, cheese, sauce, and bread is very standard fare.

But it turns out that these aren't quite as straightforward as I thought. You see, if you spread marinara sauce directly on sliced bread or a roll, as I typically do with most panini condiments, the bread turns soggy. And that's not good. After some trial and error I discovered a solution: flatbread. Sauce doesn't seep into flatbreads like naan or pita as easily as it does with cut sides of other breads. Plus, with its crust-like texture, it feels like you're eating a folded pizza. Come to think of it, I would have viewed folding a slice of cold leftover pizza and popping it into the panini press as a very viable reheating method back in my college days.

1. Heat the panini press to medium-high heat.

2. *For each sandwich:* Cut the flatbread in half across the diameter, creating two semicircles—these will become your top and bottom halves. Spread a layer of marinara on both flatbread halves. Top one half with a thin layer of cheese and arrange pepperoni slices to cover the cheese. Scatter some basil pieces over the pepperoni and top with more cheese. Close the sandwich with the other flatbread half, marinara side down.

3. Grill two panini at a time, with the lid closed, until the cheese is melted and the bread is toasted, 5 to 6 minutes.

BBQ Rib Melt Panini

▶ **Yield:** 4 panini

The next time you find yourself with leftover ribs after a barbecue, don't just reheat them—or eat them cold out of the fridge (come on, admit it!). Instead, turn them into these amazing panini. Rib meat is usually so fall-off-the-bone succulent that it really doesn't need anything more than a simple roll to make a great sandwich. That said, I'm pretty sure that if you take me up on the suggestion of including a pile of grilled onions and creamy smoked Gouda into the mix, you won't be the least bit disappointed.

1. Heat the panini press to medium-high heat.

2. Brush vegetable oil over both sides of the onion rounds. Set the onions on the grill, close the lid, and grill them until they're tender and grill marks appear, 4 to 6 minutes.

3. *For each sandwich:* Spread butter on two slices of bread to flavor the outside of the sandwich. Flip over one slice of bread and layer on the grilled onions, rib meat, and smoked Gouda. Close the sandwich with the other slice of bread, buttered side up.

4. Grill two panini at a time, with the lid closed, until the cheese is melted and the bread is toasted, 4 to 5 minutes.

1 tablespoon (15 ml) vegetable oil

1 medium-size onion, sliced crosswise into ½-inch- (1.3 cm) thick rounds (rings intact)

4 tablespoons (½ stick, or 55 g) butter, at room temperature

8 slices sourdough or other rustic white bread, sliced from a dense bakery loaf

8 ounces (225 g) barbecued pork rib meat, removed from the bone

4 ounces (115 g) smoked Gouda cheese, sliced

Cubano Panini

▶ **Yield:** 4 panini

MARINATED PORK
¼ cup (60 ml) extra-virgin olive oil
Juice of 1 orange (about ¼ cup [60 ml])
Juice of 1 lime (about 2 tablespoons [28 ml])
Juice of 1 lemon (about 2 tablespoons [28 ml])
¼ cup (4 g) chopped fresh cilantro
2 garlic cloves, minced
1 serrano chile, seeded and minced
¼ teaspoon ground cumin
4 boneless ½ inch (1.3cm) thick pork chops (about 8 ounces [225 g]; see Note)
½ teaspoon coarse salt
¼ teaspoon freshly ground black pepper

PANINI
1 French baguette, cut into 4 portions, or 4 mini baguettes
4 tablespoons (44 g) yellow mustard
8 ounces (225 g) sliced ham
¼ cup (36 g) dill pickle slices
8 ounces (225 g) Swiss cheese, sliced

Once upon a time, I used to work up the street from Porto's, a bustling, family-owned Cuban restaurant in Glendale, California, and what I enjoyed more than anything was their traditional Cuban sandwich. Slow-roasted pork, sliced ham, Swiss cheese, pickles, and mustard pressed on baguette-like Cuban bread—Cubanos rank among my absolute favorites.

If I happen to have roast pork on hand, it's the best for making Cubano-style panini. But for a quicker option, I simply marinate thin-sliced boneless pork chops in the same zesty citrus marinade that I use for Citrus-Marinated Grilled Chicken (page 48) and grill them on the panini press in just a minute or two.

1. *Marinated Pork:* Combine the oil, citrus juices, cilantro, garlic, chile, and cumin in a large zipper-top plastic bag. Add the pork, seal the bag, and roll the pork around a bit in the marinade to coat it well. Marinate the pork in the refrigerator for 2 to 4 hours.

2. Heat the panini press to medium-high heat. If your panini press comes with a removable drip tray, make sure it is in place (see page 12).

3. Remove the pork from the marinade (discard the remaining marinade) and blot the excess liquid from the meat with paper towels. Season both sides of the meat with salt and pepper.

4. Transfer the seasoned meat to the grill and close the lid. Grill the pork until it's cooked to an internal temperature of 145°F (63°C), 1 to 2 minutes.

5. *Panini:* Unplug the grill, carefully clean the grates, and then reheat the panini press to medium-high heat.

6. *For each sandwich:* Slice off the domed top of a baguette portion to create a flat grilling surface. Split the baguette to create top and bottom halves. Spread 1 tablespoon (11 g) mustard inside both baguette halves. Top the bottom half with a piece of grilled pork, followed by some ham, pickles, and cheese. Close the sandwich with the top baguette half.

7. Grill two panini at a time, with the lid closed, until the cheese is melted and the baguettes are toasted, 4 to 5 minutes.

NOTE: I can often find thin-sliced pork chops in the grocery store, but when I can't, I just ask the butcher to cut them for me.

Pork Tenderloin, Caramelized Pear, and Cheddar Panini

▶ **Yield:** 4 panini

Apples and pears have got to be the most versatile panini ingredients that I grill with. Their flavors naturally complement pork, chicken, turkey, and even beef. They also pair well with a huge variety of cheeses, including cheddar, Brie, goat cheese, and—my favorite—Manchego. Mix and match all of those together and—boom!—apples and pears turn out to be real workhorses.

Caramelized pears with pork tenderloin and sharp aged cheddar is a winning sweet-and-savory combination. Grill it on raisin bread and just watch all of those flavors go to work.

1. *Caramelized Pear:* Melt the butter in a large skillet over high heat. Add the pear and sugar and cook, stirring occasionally, until the slices are tender, with a browned caramelized crust on the outside, 4 to 6 minutes. Transfer the pears to a plate.

2. *Panini:* Heat the panini press to medium-high heat.

3. *For each sandwich:* Spread butter on two slices of bread to flavor the outside of the sandwich. Flip over one slice of bread and top it with cheese, Caramelized Pears, sliced pork tenderloin, and more cheese. Close the sandwich with the other slice of bread, buttered side up.

4. Grill two panini at a time, with the lid closed, until the cheese is melted and the bread is toasted, 4 to 6 minutes.

NOTE: Don't make your pear slices too thin or they will turn mushy when you cook them—aim for somewhere between ¼ inch (6 mm) and ½ inch (1.3 cm) thick.

CARAMELIZED PEAR
½ tablespoon butter
1 medium-size ripe, firm pear (such as Bosc), peeled, cored, and sliced (see Note)
½ teaspoon sugar

PANINI
4 tablespoons (½ stick, or 55 g) butter, at room temperature
8 slices raisin bread, sliced from a dense bakery loaf
4 ounces (115 g) sharp cheddar cheese, sliced
8 ounces (225 g) Sweet and Smoky Grilled Pork Tenderloin Medallions (page 73) or other leftover cooked pork, sliced

Pork Tenderloin, Apple Butter, and Provolone Panini

▶ **Yield:** 4 panini

4 tablespoons (½ stick, or 55 g) butter, at room temperature

8 slices of rustic white bread, sliced from a dense bakery loaf

4 ounces (115 g) provolone cheese, sliced

8 ounces (225 g) Sweet and Smoky Grilled Pork Tenderloin Medallions (page 73) or other leftover cooked pork, sliced

4 tablespoons (68 g) apple butter

Pork and apples—it's a classic sweet-and-savory combination that I just can't get enough of. As you've probably noticed, I use sliced apples quite often in panini, but I also appreciate the more concentrated (and spreadable) flavor that comes from apple butter. You'll find that my Sweet and Smoky Grilled Pork Tenderloin Medallions—with brown sugar and smoked paprika in the spice paste—work especially well with the apple butter and smoky provolone in these panini.

1. Heat the panini press to medium-high heat.

2. *For each sandwich:* Spread butter on two slices of bread to flavor the outside of the sandwich. Flip over one slice of bread and top it with cheese, sliced pork tenderloin, apple butter, and more cheese. Close the sandwich with the other slice of bread, buttered-side up.

3. Grill two panini at a time, with the lid closed, until the cheese is melted and the bread is toasted, 4 to 6 minutes.

Grilled Bacon

▶ **Yield:** 6 strips

You won't believe how easy it is to grill bacon on a panini press. It takes less time than frying or baking, and it's the perfect option on hot summer days when you don't want to stand over a stove or turn on the oven.

1. Heat the panini press to medium-high heat. If your panini press comes with a removable drip tray, make sure it is in place (see page 12).

2. Arrange as many bacon slices as will fit neatly on your grill, without overlapping. Depending on the size of your grill, you may need to trim the bacon to fit.

3. If you have a grill that allows you to adjust the height of the upper plate, set it to just barely graze the surface of bacon and not fully press the strips. Close the lid and grill the bacon until it's cooked through and crispy, 10 to 13 minutes, depending on the thickness of your bacon.

6 strips of uncooked bacon

Grilled Pork Bánh Mì

▶ **Yield:** 4 sandwiches

MARINATED GRILLED PORK

- 3 tablespoons (45 ml) fish sauce
- 2 tablespoons (40 g) honey
- 1 tablespoon (15 ml) vegetable oil
- ½ teaspoon sesame oil
- 1 tablespoon (15 g) packed dark brown sugar
- 2 tablespoons (28 ml) reduced-sodium soy sauce
- 2 garlic cloves, minced
- ½ teaspoon grated fresh ginger
- ½ teaspoon freshly ground black pepper
- 1 pound (455 g) pork tenderloin, sliced into ½-inch (1.3 cm) thick medallions

BÁNH MÌ

- 1 soft French baguette, cut into 4 portions, or 4 mini baguettes
- 4 tablespoons (60 g) mayonnaise
- 1 recipe Pickled Daikon and Carrot (recipe follows)
- 2 jalapeño peppers, seeded and thinly sliced lengthwise
- A handful of fresh cilantro

When Vietnamese *bánh mì* sandwiches first began hitting the mainstream foodie consciousness, my husband must have sought out every *bánh mì* shop nearby to taste what all the hype over a $3 sandwich was about. Each time, he'd text me something like, "Found a *bánh mì* place in San Marcos. Got the pork. SO GOOD." Once I finally had the opportunity to do some *bánh mì* scouting of my own I, too, was reeled in by the tender marinated meat and all of the mouthwatering condiments that filled the soft, warm baguette.

I adapted the succulent pork marinade for the *bánh mì* from a recipe on Food52.com.

1. *Marinated Grilled Pork:* Whisk together the fish sauce, honey, vegetable and sesame oils, dark brown sugar, soy sauce, garlic, ginger, and black pepper in a small bowl, dissolving the honey and dark brown sugar.

2. Place a few pork tenderloin medallions between two sheets of plastic wrap and use a meat pounder or rolling pin to flatten them to a ¼-inch (6 mm) thickness. Repeat with the remaining pork medallions. Place the flattened pork medallions in a zipper-top plastic bag and pour in the marinade. Seal the bag and shake it around a bit to fully coat the pork. Marinate the pork in the refrigerator for 30 minutes.

3. Heat the panini press to medium-high heat.

4. Working in batches, grill the pork, with the lid closed, until it's cooked through, about 2 minutes. Use tongs to transfer the meat to a plate and tent the plate with foil to keep it warm.

5. *For each bánh mì:* Split a baguette portion without cutting all the way through (leave a hinge intact). Spread 1 tablespoon (14 g) mayonnaise on the bottom half of each baguette. Fill each sandwich with a piece of grilled pork, Pickled Daikon and Carrot, jalapeños, and cilantro.

Pickled Daikon and Carrot

▶ **Yield:** About 1 cup (45 g)

It wouldn't be *bánh mì* without the crisp sweet-and-sour bite of pickled vegetables in the mix. Double the recipe to keep some on hand for snacking!

¼ cup (60 ml) distilled white vinegar
¼ cup (50 g) sugar
¼ cup (60 ml) water
½ teaspoon coarse salt
1 medium-size carrot, peeled and cut into matchstick strips
½ of a medium-size daikon radish, peeled and cut into matchstick strips

Whisk together the vinegar, sugar, water, and salt in a medium-size bowl. Add the carrots and daikon. Cover the bowl and refrigerate it for at least 4 hours.
The pickles will keep, covered in the refrigerator, for several weeks.

Beer-Grilled Bratwursts

▶ **Yield:** 4 servings

2 tablespoons (28 g) butter
2 medium-size onions,
   1 halved and sliced into
   strips (French-cut) and
   1 sliced crosswise into
   ½-inch (1.3 cm) thick
   rands (rings intact)
4 uncooked bratwursts
   (about 1 pound [455 g])
2 to 3 bottles or cans of
   beer (12 ounce, or
   355 ml each) (see Note)
1 teaspoon vegetable oil
4 bratwurst buns or hot dog
   buns, toasted if desired
1 cup (142 g) sauerkraut
German-style or Dijon
   mustard, to taste

Don't let rain put a damper on your sports watching (and eating) plans. Simmer your brats in a pot full of beer and onions on the stove, grill some onions on the panini press, and then crisp up the brats on the grill—you won't even need to turn them.

Beyond bratwurst, you can grill pretty much any precooked sausage on the panini press—hot dogs, chicken sausages, breakfast links, you name it. The key is to keep the heat on the lower side to avoid bursting the casings. If your panini press doesn't allow you to adjust the heat, you may want to test it out on just one sausage at first.

1. Melt the butter in a Dutch oven or large pot over medium-high heat. Add the French-cut onion slices to the pot, and cook, stirring occasionally, until they're softened, 4 to 5 minutes. Add the bratwursts and enough beer to cover them. Bring the beer to a boil, and then immediately reduce the heat to a simmer. Continue cooking the bratwursts for another 12 minutes, or until the internal temperature reaches 160°F (71°C). They will feel denser to the touch when they're done—but don't slice into them or all of the juices will escape!

2. While the bratwursts are simmering, heat the panini press to medium-high heat. Brush vegetable oil over both sides of the onion rounds and grill them, with the lid closed, until they're tender and grill marks appear, 4 to 6 minutes. Transfer the onions to a plate.

3. Reduce the heat on the panini press to medium-low. With a pair of tongs, remove the bratwursts from the beer, set them on the panini press, and close the lid. Grill the bratwursts until dark grill marks appear, 4 to 5 minutes.

4. Serve the bratwursts on buns with grilled onions, sauerkraut, and mustard.

NOTE: Many people suggest using dark beer for braising bratwurst, but at the end of the day you're best off choosing whichever kind you like to drink—or, more accurately, smell, because the aromas of simmering beer are about to fill your kitchen!

Sweet and Smoky Grilled Pork Tenderloin Medallions

▶ **Yield:** 4 servings

True to its name, this recipe is sweet and smoky—and extremely easy to prepare on a weeknight. I make a quick spice paste, starring brown sugar and smoked paprika, and let it soak into the pork while I prepare a simple side dish. Then, after just 2 minutes on the panini press, the meat is juicy, flavorful . . . and done!

Turn your leftovers from this dish into Pork Tenderloin, Caramelized Pear, and Cheddar Panini (page 67) or Pork Tenderloin, Apple Butter, and Provolone Panini (page 68).

1 tablespoon (15 g) packed brown sugar
1 teaspoon coarse salt
1 teaspoon smoked paprika
¼ teaspoon dry mustard
¼ teaspoon garlic powder
¼ teaspoon freshly ground black pepper
A dash of cayenne pepper
2 teaspoons vegetable oil
1 pork tenderloin (1 pound, or 455 g)

1. In a small bowl, mix the brown sugar, salt, smoked paprika, dry mustard, garlic powder, black pepper, and cayenne until they're well combined. Stir in the vegetable oil to form a paste.

2. Cut the pork tenderloin crosswise into 8 pieces, each about 1 inch (2.5 cm) thick. Use the heel of your hand to press each piece into a ½-inch (1.3 cm) thick medallion.

3. Rub ¼ to ½ teaspoon of the spice paste over the top and bottom of each pork medallion. Let the pork sit at room temperature for 30 minutes to allow the flavors to seep in.

4. Heat the panini press to high heat. If your panini press comes with a removable drip tray, make sure it is in place (see page 12).

5. Working in batches if necessary, place the pork medallions on the grill and close the lid. Grill the pork until it's cooked to an internal temperature of 145°F (63°C), about 2 minutes. Allow the pork to rest for 5 minutes before slicing.

THE BUTCHER'S BEST

Beef and Lamb on the Panini Press

Roast Beef, Cheddar, and Arugula Salad Panini

▶ **Yield:** 4 panini

I toss together an arugula salad here for a punch of peppery flavor and acidity. Along with spicy whole-grain mustard, it's the perfect match for the richness of the roast beef and cheddar cheese.

1. Heat the panini press to medium-high heat.

2. Place the arugula in a medium-size bowl and toss it with about a tablespoon (15 ml) of vinaigrette—more or less, depending on your taste.

3. *For each sandwich:* Spread butter on two slices of bread to flavor the outside of the sandwich. Flip over one slice of bread and top it with cheese, some arugula salad, roast beef, and more cheese. Flip over the other slice of bread and spread a thin layer of mustard on the other side. Close the sandwich with the other slice of bread, buttered-side up.

4. Grill two panini at a time, with the lid closed, until the cheese is melted and the bread is toasted, 4 to 5 minutes.

- 2 cups (40 g) baby arugula
- 1 tablespoon (15 ml) White Balsamic Vinaigrette (see below), or to taste
- 4 tablespoons (½ stick, or 55 g) butter, at room temperature
- 8 slices of rustic white bread, sliced from a dense bakery loaf
- 4 ounces (115 g) sharp cheddar cheese, sliced
- 8 ounces (225 g) thinly sliced roast beef
- 2 tablespoons (30 g) whole-grain mustard

White Balsamic Vinaigrette

▶ **Yield:** About ¾ cup (175 ml)

1. In a small bowl, whisk together the vinegar, shallots, Dijon mustard, salt, and pepper. While still whisking, slowly drizzle in the olive oil.

2. You can keep any extra white balsamic vinaigrette in the refrigerator for up to a week. Allow the dressing to come to room temperature and give it a good stir before using it next.

- 3 tablespoons (45 ml) white balsamic vinegar (you can substitute regular balsamic)
- 2 teaspoons chopped shallots
- ½ teaspoon Dijon mustard
- ½ teaspoon coarse salt
- ½ teaspoon freshly ground black pepper
- ½ cup extra-virgin olive oil

Hawaiian Flank Steak Teriyaki Panini

▶ **Yield:** 4 panini

**MARINATED FLANK
STEAK**
3 tablespoons (45 ml) mirin
3 tablespoons (45 ml)
   reduced-sodium soy
   sauce
3 tablespoons (45 ml) sake
1 tablespoon (15 ml)
   packed dark brown sugar
2 teaspoons grated fresh
   ginger
1 flank steak (1 to 1½
   pound, 455 to 680 g)

TERIYAKI MAYONNAISE
½ cup (115 g) mayonnaise
1 tablespoon (15 ml)
   reduced-sodium soy
   sauce
1 tablespoon (15 ml) mirin
1 teaspoon grated fresh
   ginger

PANINI
1 ciabatta loaf, cut into 4
   portions,
   or 4 ciabatta rolls
8 pineapple rings, canned
   or fresh,
   patted dry with paper
   towels
¼ cup (4 g) chopped fresh
   cilantro
1 recipe Crispy Fried
   Onions (page 77)

Believe it or not, I built these panini around the sweet Maui onions rather than the steak. Just the thought of Maui onions takes me right back to my honeymoon and Kula Lodge, the dark wood restaurant perched on a hillside in the island's upcountry, where they served my husband and me Maui onion soup—with a side of sweeping views of the Pacific. To bring these nostalgia-inducing onions into my sandwiches, I fry them nice and crispy and, in keeping with the Hawaiian mood, match them with teriyaki-marinated flank steak, grilled pineapple, cilantro, and teriyaki mayonnaise. Since there's no cheese to melt on these panini, I simply toast the bread on the panini press rather than grill the sandwiches.

1. *Marinated Flank Steak:* Whisk together the mirin, soy sauce, sake, dark brown sugar, and ginger in a small bowl until the sugar has dissolved. Place the flank steak in a large zipper-top plastic bag and pour in the marinade. Seal the bag and rotate the steak around a bit to make sure the marinade fully coats it. Marinate the steak in the refrigerator for at least 4 hours and up to 24 hours.

2. *Teriyaki Mayonnaise:* In a small bowl, whisk together the mayonnaise, soy sauce, mirin, and ginger until well combined and smooth. Refrigerate the mayonnaise until you're ready to use it.

3. *Panini:* Heat the panini press to medium-high heat.

4. Grill two ciabatta portions at a time, cut sides down, until they're toasted and grill marks appear, about 2 minutes. Set aside.

5. Grill the pineapple slices, in batches if necessary, until they're caramelized and dark grill marks appear, 3 to 4 minutes. Carefully scrape the excess pineapple juices from the grates with a grill scraper.

6. Raise the heat on the panini press to high. If your panini press comes with a removable drip tray, make sure it is in place (see page 12).

7. Remove the flank steak from the plastic bag, discarding the marinade. Place the steak on the grill, close the lid, and grill the steak to your desired doneness, 8 to 10 minutes for medium (137°F [58°C]). Allow the steak to rest on a cutting board for 10 minutes before slicing it thinly across the grain. Meanwhile, unplug the grill and while it's still hot, carefully scrape down the grates with your grill scraper to remove any stuck-on bits of meat.

8. *For each sandwich:* Spread 1 tablespoon (14 g) Teriyaki Mayonnaise on the cut sides of a toasted ciabatta portion. On the bottom half, lay 2 pineapple rings, some sliced steak, a sprinkling of chopped cilantro, and some Crsipy Fried Onions. Close the panini with the top ciabatta half.

Crispy Fried Onions

▶ **Yield:** About 1 cup (55 g)

I wish I didn't love these onions so much. By the time the last batch is done, I've often already polished off the first batch! Snacking aside, these crispy onions are perfect for adding a savory crunch to beef and vegetable panini or as a garnish for dishes like Grilled Rib-Eye Steak (page 93) or Grilled Salmon Sandwiches with BBQ Rémoulade (page 98).

> ½ cup (60 ml) vegetable oil
> ½ cup (63 g) all-purpose flour
> ½ teaspoon coarse salt
> 1 sweet onion (such as Maui, Walla Walla, or Vidalia), halved and thinly sliced

1. Heat the vegetable oil in a medium-size skillet over medium-high heat until a pinch of flour sizzles on contact.

2. Combine the flour and salt in a shallow bowl and toss the onions around in the mixture until they're well coated. Carefully add the onions to the hot oil—in batches if necessary to avoid overcrowding the pan—and cook them, stirring occasionally, until they are golden brown and crisp, 4 to 5 minutes. Use a slotted spoon to transfer the onions to a plate lined with paper towels to drain.

Chimichurri Skirt Steak Panini with Provolone and Sun-Dried Tomatoes

▶ **Yield:** 4 panini

1 French baguette, cut into
   4 portions, or
   4 mini baguettes
½ cup (120 ml) Chimichurri
   Sauce (page 90)
1 recipe Chimichurri Skirt
   Steak (page 90)
¼ cup (28 g) thinly sliced
   oil-packed sun-dried
   tomatoes
4 ounces (115 g) provolone
   cheese, sliced

Once you've tried steak with Chimichurri Sauce, it's a natural inclination to want to make a sandwich out of it. Not only do the tender slices of steak combine beautifully with sharp melted cheese, but the zesty, garlicky Argentine sauce is a real treat when it soaks into bread. Here, I've chosen to use a sturdy French baguette that can absorb all of that sauce without sacrificing its firm texture. A few sun-dried tomatoes scattered over the top bring a sweet burst to each bite.

Use Leftovers: You can make these panini with any leftover steak you have on hand and substitute pesto for the Chimichurri Sauce.

1. Heat the panini press to medium-high heat.

2. *For each sandwich:* Slice off the domed top of a baguette portion to create a flat grilling surface. Split the baguette to create top and bottom halves. Spoon 1 tablespoon (15 ml) Chimichurri Sauce inside each half. On the bottom half, layer sliced steak, sun-dried tomatoes, and cheese. Close the sandwich with the top baguette half.

3. Grill two panini at a time, with the lid closed, until the cheese is melted and the baguettes are toasted, 5 to 7 minutes.

Tri-Tip French Dip Panini au Jus

▶ **Yield:** 4 panini

I love to grill a nicely marbled tri-tip steak on the panini press and pile it on a baguette with horseradish cheddar and sweet Caramelized Onions. Since grilling doesn't yield quite the same amount of juices as oven-roasting the beef, I simply simmer my own broth-based *jus* on the stove.

Short on Time? You can use regular deli-sliced roast beef in place of the grilled tri-tip.

1. *Tri-tip:* Heat the panini press to medium-high heat. If your press comes with a removable drip tray, ensure it is in place (see page 12).

2. Season the steak with salt and pepper. Set the steak on the grill, close the lid, and grill it to your desired doneness, 20 to 22 minutes for medium (137°F [58°C]).

3. Transfer the steak to a cutting board. Allow it to rest for at least 10 minutes before slicing it thinly across the grain. You can either clean off your grill at this point or use the extra flavor those leftover juices will add to your panini when it comes time to grill them.

4. *Jus:* While the steak is grilling, prepare your *jus*. In a medium-size saucepan, melt the butter over medium heat. Add the shallot and cook, stirring occasionally, until softened, about 2 minutes. Add the garlic and cook until fragrant and just beginning to brown, another 30 to 60 seconds. Pour in the beef broth and add the bay leaf, thyme, coriander, celery seeds, and cloves. Bring the broth to a simmer and continue simmering for 15 minutes to allow the flavors to blend. Remove the *jus* from the heat and season with salt and pepper to taste. Discard the bay leaf and cover the pan to keep the broth warm.

5. *Panini:* Reheat the panini press to medium-high heat.

6. *For each sandwich:* Slice off the domed top of a baguette portion to create a flat grilling surface. Split the baguette to create top and bottom halves. Inside the bottom half, layer on cheese, caramelized onions, tri-tip, and more cheese. Close the sandwich with the top baguette half.

7. Grill two panini at a time, with the lid closed, until the cheese is melted and the baguettes are toasted, 5 to 7 minutes. Serve each sandwich with a little bowl of warm jus for dipping.

TRI-TIP
1 tri-tip steak (1½ pound, or 680 g)
1 teaspoon coarse salt
½ teaspoon freshly ground black pepper

PANINI
1 French baguette, cut into 4 portions, or 4 mini baguettes
4 ounces (115 g) horseradish cheddar cheese, thinly sliced
1 cup (195 g) Caramelized Onions (page 26)

JUS
1 tablespoon (14 g) unsalted butter
1 shallot, thinly sliced
2 garlic cloves, minced
3 cups (700 ml) low-sodium beef broth
1 bay leaf
1 teaspoon dried thyme
½ teaspoon ground coriander
½ teaspoon celery seeds
A pinch of ground cloves
Coarse salt and freshly ground black pepper

Green Chile Steak Melt Panini

▶ **Yield:** 4 panini

At the end of a long day of kite flying and butterfly chasing on a family vacation in Santa Barbara, I ordered a fantastic spicy steak sandwich at a restaurant that evening. It was a Southwestern take on the classic cheese steak, made with thinly sliced steak, chiles, onions, pepper Jack cheese, and chipotle *crema* on a baguette. The concept went straight into the Notes app on my iPhone to remind me to re-create it when I got back home. For my version, I caramelized the onions to bring in more sweetness and dialed down the spice level a touch by using Monterey Jack rather than pepper Jack. Lastly, I converted the chipotle *crema* to a chipotle mayonnaise (which still has a touch of cooling sour cream in it).

Use Leftovers: If you've got leftover steak on hand, go ahead and use it here instead of grilling a new steak.

1. Heat the panini press to high heat. If your panini press comes with a removable drip tray, make sure it is in place (see page 12).

2. Season the steak generously with salt and pepper.

3. Grill the steak, with the lid closed, to your desired doneness, 10 to 15 minutes for medium (137°F [58°C]). Transfer the steak to a cutting board and let it rest for 10 minutes before slicing it very thinly across the grain. Meanwhile, unplug the grill and while it's still hot, scrape down the grates with a grill scraper. Let the grill cool and clean the grates.

4. Reheat the panini press to medium-high heat.

5. *For each sandwich:* Split the ciabatta to create top and bottom halves. Spread 1 tablespoon (14 g) Chipotle Mayonnaise inside each half. On the bottom half, layer cheese, sliced steak, Caramelized Onions, chiles, and more cheese. Close the sandwich with the top half.

6. Grill two panini at a time, with the lid closed, until the cheese is melted and the rolls are toasted, 5 to 7 minutes.

(Continued on next page)

---

1 New York strip steak
  (1 pound, or 455 g)
Coarse salt and freshly
  ground black pepper
1 ciabatta loaf, cut into
  4 portions, or
  4 ciabatta rolls
1 recipe Chipotle Mayon-
  naise (recipe follows)
4 ounces (115 g) Monterey
  Jack cheese, sliced
1 cup (195 g) Caramelized
  Onions (page 26)
1 can (7 ounces, or 200 g)
  roasted whole green chiles, drained and chopped

Green Chile Steak Melt Panini

(continued)

Chipotle Mayonnaise

▶ **Yield:** About ¹/₂ cup, (115 g)

Get ready for a Southwestern kick! Smoky chipotle peppers (which are ripe jalapeños that have been smoke-dried) bring fiery flavor to this spread, which I adore on everything from steak to turkey to salmon. The sour cream cools things off, keeping the spice level in check. If you find it too hot for your taste, just add more sour cream.

½ cup (115 g) mayonnaise
1 tablespoon (15 g) sour cream
1 tablespoon (3 g) finely chopped chives
1 canned chipotle in adobo sauce, plus
   1½ teaspoons of the adobo sauce
1 teaspoon freshly squeezed lemon juice
Coarse salt and freshly ground black pepper

Combine the mayonnaise, sour cream, chives, chipotle, adobo sauce, and lemon juice in a food processor or blender. Process or blend until smooth. Season the mayonnaise with salt and pepper to taste. Cover the bowl and refrigerate the mayonnaise until you are ready to serve it.

Cheese Steak Panini

▶ **Yield:** 4 panini

A lot of folks swear that for a truly authentic Philly cheese steak, you've got to go to Philadelphia—and I'm inclined to believe them. But I still like to make my own Philly-style cheese steaks at home, grilling a juicy flatiron steak, slicing it thin, and piling it on a roll with grilled onions, sharp provolone, and hot peppers.

1. *Grilled Steak:* Heat the panini press to high. If your panini press comes with a removable drip tray, make sure it is in place (see page 12).

2. Season both sides of the steak with salt, garlic powder, and pepper. Grill the steak, with the lid closed, to your desired doneness, 5 to 7 minutes for medium (137°F [58°F]).

3. Transfer the steak to a cutting board and let it rest for 10 minutes before slicing it very thinly across the grain. Meanwhile, unplug the panini press and while it's still hot, carefully scrape down the grates with a grill scraper to remove any stuck-on bits of meat. Allow the grill to cool and clean the grates.

4. *Panini:* Reheat the panini press to medium-high heat.

5. Brush oil on both sides of the onion slices and season them with salt and pepper. Grill the onions until they're tender and dark grill marks appear, 6 to 8 minutes. Transfer the onions to a bowl and toss them to break up the rings.

6. *For each sandwich:* Split a ciabatta portion to create top and bottom halves. Pile some of the grilled onion rings inside the bottom half and add sliced steak, hot peppers, and cheese. Close the sandwich with the top half.

7. Grill two panini at a time, with the lid closed, until the cheese is melted and the ciabatta is toasted, 5 to 6 minutes.

GRILLED STEAK
- 1 flatiron or top blade steak (1 pound, or 455 g)
- 1 teaspoon coarse salt
- 1 teaspoon garlic powder
- ½ teaspoon freshly ground black pepper

PANINI
- 1 tablespoon (15 ml) vegetable oil
- 1 medium-size onion, cut crosswise into ½-inch (1.3 cm) thick slices (rings intact)
- Coarse salt and freshly ground black pepper
- 1 ciabatta loaf, cut into 4 portions, or 4 ciabatta rolls
- 4 to 6 jarred hot Italian peppers, such as banana peppers or fried "long-hot" cayenne peppers, sliced
- 4 ounces (115 g) sharp provolone, sliced

Cheeseburger Patty Melt Panini

▶ **Yield:** 4 panini

1 tablespoon (15 ml) vegetable oil

1 medium-size onion, sliced into ½-inch (1.3 cm) thick rounds (rings intact)

1 pound (455 g) 85% lean ground beef

1 teaspoon coarse salt

½ teaspoon freshly ground black pepper

4 tablespoons (½ stick, or 55 g) butter, at room temperature

8 slices of rye bread or rustic white bread, sliced from a dense bakery loaf

4 ounces (115 g) sharp cheddar or Swiss cheese, sliced

1 recipe Thousand Island Dressing (page 86)

I might go so far as to say that a patty melt is even better than a regular burger. Grilled on rye bread and enveloped in cheese, a patty melt tends to hold its ingredients intact better than its burger counterpart. Condiments like grilled onions and Thousand Island Dressing are an insurance policy, so that on the off chance you overcook the patty, you'll still end up with a flavorful sandwich. And then there's the rye bread—bread that actually *tastes like something*—cradling your burger patty. Yup, give me a good patty melt over a regular burger any day.

1. Heat the panini press to medium-high heat. If your panini press comes with a removable drip tray, make sure it is in place (see page 12).

2. Brush vegetable oil on both sides of the onions. Grill the onions until they're tender and dark grill marks appear, 6 to 8 minutes. Transfer the grilled onions to a plate.

3. While the onions are grilling, divide the ground beef into four equal patties. Season the patties on both sides with salt and pepper. After the onions are cooked, grill the burgers to your desired doneness, 4 to 5 minutes for medium (137°F [58°F]). Carefully scrape the grates with a grill scraper to remove most of the excess grease and cooked-on bits (they don't need to be completely clean).

4. *For each sandwich:* Spread butter on two slices of bread to flavor the outside of the sandwich. Flip over one slice and top the other side with cheese, grilled onions, a burger patty, a dollop of Thousand Island Dressing, and more cheese. Close the sandwich with the other slice of bread, buttered side up.

5. Grill two panini at a time, with the lid closed, until the cheese is melted and the bread is toasted, 4 to 5 minutes.

Reuben Panini

▶ **Yield:** 4 panini

4 tablespoons (½ stick, or 55 g) butter, at room temperature
8 slices of rye bread, sliced from a dense bakery loaf
4 ounces (115 g) Swiss cheese, sliced
8 ounces (225 g) sliced corned beef
1 recipe Thousand Island Dressing (recipe follows)
½ cup (71 g) sauerkraut

Once upon a time, I asked Panini Happy readers to name their favorite sandwich. The overwhelming choice turned out to be the Reuben. It wasn't hard for me to understand why. Just the sight of all of that bright pink, salty corned beef piled on top of mouthwatering sauerkraut, with Thousand Island Dressing and melted Swiss cheese on rye . . . well, you know you're in for a flavor explosion.

There are lots of Reuben variations out there—some use turkey or pastrami instead of corned beef, some opt for Russian dressing rather than Thousand Island. This version happens to be the one I like best, especially after St. Patrick's Day, when there is leftover corned beef in the fridge.

1. Heat the panini press to medium-high heat.

2. *For each sandwich:* Spread butter on two slices of bread to flavor the outside of the sandwich. Flip over one slice and top the other side with cheese, corned beef, a dollop of Thousand Island Dressing, sauerkraut, and more cheese. Close the sandwich with the other slice of bread, buttered-side up.

3. Grill two panini at a time, with the lid closed, until the cheese is melted and the bread is toasted, 4 to 5 minutes.

½ cup (115 g) mayonnaise
2 tablespoons (30 g) ketchup
2 teaspoons sweet pickle relish
2 teaspoons Worcestershire sauce
2 teaspoons minced onion
Coarse salt and freshly ground black pepper

Thousand Island Dressing

▶ **Yield:** About ¹/₂ cup (120 g)

Classic Thousand Island Dressing is good for more than just an iceberg lettuce salad. Use this creamy, tangy condiment for everything from a spread for burgers and turkey sandwiches to a dip for shrimp.

Whisk together the mayonnaise, ketchup, pickle relish, Worcestershire sauce, and onion in a small bowl and season with salt and pepper to taste. Cover the bowl and refrigerate the dressing until you're ready to use it.

Lamb, Fig, and Goat Cheese Panini with Fennel Slaw

▶ **Yield:** 4 panini

One of the best ways I know to add crunch and acidity to a sandwich is with a slaw. Here, a simple slaw with shaved fennel tossed in lemon juice and olive oil is the perfect complement to the marinated lamb, sweet fig preserves, and creamy goat cheese.

1. Heat the panini press to medium-high heat.

2. *For each sandwich:* Slice off the domed top of a baguette portion to create a flat grilling surface. Split the baguette to create top and bottom halves. Spread 1 tablespoon (20 g) fig preserves inside the bottom half and a layer of goat cheese inside the top half. Top the preserves with Fennel Slaw and sliced lamb. Close the sandwich with the top baguette half.

3. Grill two panini at a time, with the lid closed, until the goat cheese is softened and the baguettes are toasted, 3 to 4 minutes.

1 French baguette, cut into
  4 portions, or
  4 mini baguettes
4 tablespoons (80 g) fig
  preserves
4 ounces (115 g) goat
  cheese, at room tem-
  perature, sliced into thin
  medallions
1 recipe Fennel Slaw
  (recipe follows)
8 ounces (225 g) Marinated
  Lamb Chops (page 94) or
  leftover cooked lamb or
  beef, thinly sliced

Fennel Slaw

▶ **Yield:** About 1¹/₂ cups

This slaw is a fresh, crisp, flavorful side dish in its own right, but the raw fennel and lemony dressing also bring wonderful crunch and acidity to panini.

In a medium-size bowl, whisk together the olive oil, lemon juice, and sugar. Season the dressing with a few pinches of salt and pepper to taste. Cut off the stalks and fronds from the fennel bulb and save them for another use. With a sharp knife or, ideally, a mandoline, carefully shave the fennel into very thin slices. Toss the shaved fennel with the dressing.

1 tablespoon (15 ml)
  extra-virgin olive oil
1 tablespoon (15 ml) freshly
  squeezed lemon juice
A pinch of sugar
Coarse salt and freshly
  ground black pepper
1 medium-size fennel bulb

Greek Lamb Panini with Feta, Tapenade, and Sun-Dried Tomatoes

▶ **Yield:** 4 panini

4 pita breads

4 tablespoons (32 g) olive tapenade

½ small red onion, thinly sliced

8 ounces (225 g) Marinated Lamb Chops (page 94) or leftover cooked lamb or beef, thinly sliced

8 oil-packed sun-dried tomatoes, thinly sliced

8 fresh basil leaves, roughly torn

4 ounces (115 g) crumbled feta cheese

I can add feta, olive tapenade, and sun-dried tomatoes to almost anything and be happy. These zesty Mediterranean flavors go particularly well with lamb.

1. Heat the panini press to medium-high heat.

2. *For each sandwich:* Cut a pita in half across the diameter, creating two semicircles—these will become your top and bottom halves. Spread 1 tablespoon (8 g) tapenade on one pita half. Top the tapenade with red onions, lamb, sun-dried tomatoes, basil, and feta. Close the sandwich with the other pita half.

3. Grill two panini at a time, with the lid closed, until they're heated through and the pitas are toasted, 3 to 4 minutes.

Chimichurri Skirt Steak

▶ **Yield:** 2 to 4 servings

1 skirt steak (1 pound, or
   455 g) (see Note)
Coarse salt and freshly
   ground black pepper
1 recipe Chimichurri Sauce
   (recipe follows)

I've chosen to dress this simple grilled skirt steak in chimichurri sauce, but you can always take the same steak, add your own favorite seasonings, and use it in tacos, salads, or, of course, sandwiches. You may want to double the recipe to make Chimichurri Skirt Steak Panini with Provolone and Sun-Dried Tomatoes (page 78) later in the week.

1. About 30 minutes before you're ready to grill, set the steak out at room temperature. If necessary, trim the length of the steak strips to fit your grill.

2. Heat the panini press to high heat. If your panini press comes with a removable drip tray, make sure it is in place (see page 12).

3. Pat the steak dry with paper towels, season it generously with salt and pepper, and place it on the grill. Close the lid so that the upper plate is resting on the meat.

4. Grill the steak until it's cooked to your desired doneness, 4 to 5 minutes for medium (137°F [58°F]).

5. Let the steak rest for 5 minutes before slicing it thinly across the grain, with your knife set at a 45° angle (this will give you really tender slices). Serve the steak with the Chimichurri Sauce.

NOTE: You might be able to find skirt steak in the butcher department of your regular grocery store; if not, look for it at a specialty grocer or butcher shop. Alternatively, you can substitute flank steak for this recipe.

Chimichurri Sauce

▶ **Yield:** About ³/₄ cup (175 ml)

The first time I ever tried Chimichurri Sauce I was blown away by how much fresh, herby, garlicky flavor was packed inside it. The sauce, which originated in Argentina, reminds me a bit of pesto, minus the creaminess. It's the kind of stuff that makes you start looking around your fridge and pantry for all kinds of ways to use it—bread to drizzle it on, potatoes to toss it in for a salad, vegetables to marinate in it. You don't want a single drop of this to go to waste.

1 cup (60 g) packed finely chopped fresh Italian parsley
4 garlic cloves, minced
½ cup (60 ml) extra-virgin olive oil
1 tablespoon (15 ml) red wine vinegar
1 tablespoon (15 ml) freshly squeezed lemon juice
1 tablespoon (3 g) dried oregano
1 teaspoon coarse salt
¼ teaspoon freshly ground black pepper
¼ teaspoon red pepper flakes

Combine all of the ingredients in a medium nonreactive bowl and set the sauce aside at room temperature until ready to use. You can store any leftover Chimichurri Sauce in an airtight container in the refrigerator for a day or two—just bring it back to room temperature before you serve it.

Grilled Flank Steak Fajitas

▶ **Yield:** 4 servings

3 tablespoons (45 ml)
   extra-virgin olive oil
½ cup (120 ml)
   reduced-sodium soy
   sauce
2 tablespoons (28 ml)
   freshly squeezed lime
   juice
2 tablespoons (30 ml)
   packed brown sugar
1 tablespoon (6 g) ancho
   chile powder
2 teaspoons ground cumin
1 teaspoon ground
   coriander
¼ teaspoon cayenne pepper
2 garlic cloves, minced
1 flank steak (1¼ pound, or
   570 g) (see Note)
1 medium-size onion,
   halved and sliced
1 red bell pepper, cored,
   seeded, and sliced
1 green bell pepper, cored,
   seeded, and sliced

ACCOMPANIMENTS
Warm flour tortillas
Sliced avocados
Chopped tomatoes
Sour cream
Shredded cheddar and/or
   Monterey Jack cheese
Salsa

Fajitas are high on my list of go-to weeknight meals. Everyone in my house customizes what goes into their tortillas, so we're all happy. The hardest part is remembering to marinate the meat ahead of time so all of those fabulous Southwestern flavors have a chance to sink in. The 20 minutes that it takes for the steak to grill and rest gives me ample time to sauté some bell peppers and onions and assemble all of our fixings. Yay, fajita night!

1. In a small bowl, whisk together 2 tablespoons (28 ml) of the olive oil, the soy sauce, lime juice, brown sugar, ancho chile powder, cumin, coriander, cayenne, and garlic.

2. Place the flank steak in a large zipper-top bag. Pour in the marinade and seal the bag. Gently squeeze the steak around in the bag a bit to ensure the marinade coats it well. Transfer the bag to the refrigerator and marinate the steak for 8 hours.

3. Heat the panini press to high heat. If your panini press comes with a removable drip tray, make sure it is in place (see page 12).

4. Remove the steak from the marinade (discard the remaining marinade) and pat it dry with paper towels. Lay the steak on the grill, close the lid, and cook the steak to your desired doneness, 8 to 10 minutes for medium (137°F [58°F]). Let the steak rest on a cutting board for 10 minutes before slicing it thinly across the grain.

5. Meanwhile, heat a large skillet over medium high heat. Swirl in the remaining 1 tablespoon (15 ml) of olive oil and add the onion and bell peppers. Cook the vegetables, stirring occasionally, until they're tender, about 10 minutes.

6. Serve the steak, and sautéed onions, and bell peppers in warm flour tortillas. Dress up the fajitas however you like, with accompaniments such as sliced avocado, chopped tomatoes, sour cream, shredded cheese, and salsa.

NOTE: Depending on the size of your grill, you may need to trim the steak in order for it to fit.

Grilled Rib-Eye Steak

▶ **Yield:** 2 servings

Most often I grill with big-flavor marinades, but once in a while I yearn for the simplicity of the salt-and-pepper-only route. Especially when I've got a thick, wonderfully marbled cut of meat like a rib-eye, I want the natural richness of the meat to really shine through.

1. Pat the steak dry with paper towels, rub olive oil all over it, and season it generously with black pepper. Set it out at room temperature for about 30 minutes.

2. Heat the panini press to high heat. If your panini press comes with a removable drip tray, make sure it is in place (see page 12).

3. Season the steak generously with coarse salt and set it on the grill. Close the lid so that it's resting right on top of the meat. Don't bother adjusting the height of the upper plate (if your grill has that feature). The steak will shrink a little as it cooks, and if your grill height is in a fixed position, it will likely lose contact with the meat.

4. Grill the steak to your desired doneness, 12 to 15 minutes for medium (137°F [58°F]). If your steak happens to weigh more or less than 1¼ pounds (570 g), just adjust your grilling time. I can't underscore enough how helpful an instant-read thermometer is for grilling to the right temperature.

5. Let the steak rest for 10 minutes on a cutting board before slicing it thinly across the grain.

1 rib-eye steak (1¼ pound, or 570 g), about 1½ inches (3.8 cm) thick
1 tablespoon (15 ml) extra-virgin olive oil
Freshly ground black pepper
Coarse salt

Marinated Lamb Chops

▶ **Yield:** 4 servings

¼ cup (60 ml) extra-virgin olive oil

¼ cup (60 ml) balsamic vinegar

2 teaspoons dried rosemary

2 garlic cloves, minced

1 teaspoon Dijon mustard

½ teaspoon freshly ground black pepper

2 pounds (900 g) boneless lamb shoulder chops, about 1 inch (1.3 cm) thick (see Note)

½ teaspoon coarse salt

What do you mean *he don't eat no meat*?!" Aunt Voula reacts in disbelief to Toula's vegetarian fiancé in *My Big Fat Greek Wedding*. Everyone around them stops their conversations and stares. "That's okay. That's okay. I make lamb!"

Thanks to that hilarious movie, I can't help but think to myself "I make lamb" whenever I'm getting ready to grill these chops. Not only are they an incredibly easy weeknight main dish—after marinating in the refrigerator overnight they grill in less than 20 minutes—but the juicy, flavorful meat (sorry, Aunt Voula!) is perfect for sandwiches. Use any leftovers for Lamb, Fig, and Goat Cheese Panini with Fennel Slaw (page 87), or Greek Lamb Panini with Feta, Tapenade, and Sun-Dried Tomatoes (page 88).

1. In a small bowl, whisk together the olive oil, balsamic vinegar, rosemary, garlic, mustard, and black pepper. Pour the marinade into a large zipper-top plastic bag. Add the lamb chops and gently massage the marinade into the meat. Seal the bag and marinate the lamb in the refrigerator for at least 4 hours and preferably overnight.

2. Heat the panini press to high heat. If your panini press comes with a removable drip tray, make sure it is in place (see page 12).

3. Remove the lamb from the marinade (discard the remaining marinade) and pat it dry with paper towels. Season the lamb chops on both sides with salt. Working in batches, grill the lamb, with the lid closed, until it's cooked to an internal temperature of 145°F (63°F), 6 to 8 minutes. Allow the lamb to rest for 10 minutes on a cutting board before slicing it thinly across the grain.

NOTE: Shoulder chops are usually sold boneless, but if you can find only bone-in chops, buy slightly more than 2 pounds (900 g). Bone-in chops may take a little longer to cook—be sure to check the temperature with a meat thermometer.

GIFTS FROM THE SEA

Seafood on the Panini Press

Greek Shrimp Panini with Pesto, Feta, and Sun-Dried Tomatoes

▶ **Yield:** 4 panini

The trouble with making sandwiches with shrimp is that the little guys have a tendency to slip and slide around a bit. I've played around with a lot of different shrimp panini concepts and I finally figured out the key to making them work: a wide berth of bread. Give shrimp a little wiggle room—either on a dense sliced bread or a wider ciabatta—and they play nicely with your other ingredients. Which is a very good thing, because these flavorful panini deserve to be grilled as often as possible.

1. Heat the panini press to medium-high heat.

2. In a medium-size bowl, toss the shrimp in the oil to coat them. Season the shrimp lightly with salt and pepper.

3. Arrange the shrimp in a single layer on the grill (work in batches if necessary) and close the lid. Grill the shrimp until they're cooked through and opaque, about 2 minutes. Unplug the grill and, while it's still hot, carefully scrape off any cooked-on shrimp with a grill scraper. Once the grill is cool, clean the grates.

4. Reheat the panini press to medium-high heat.

5. *For each sandwich:* Split a ciabatta portion to create top and bottom halves. Spread a thin layer of pesto inside each ciabatta half. On the bottom half layer shrimp, feta, sun-dried tomatoes, and basil. Close the sandwich with the top ciabatta half.

6. Grill two panini at a time, with the lid closed, until the cheese is softened and the ciabatta is toasted, 3 to 4 minutes.

8 ounces (225 g) raw medium-size shrimp, peeled and deveined

2 teaspoons vegetable oil

Coarse salt and freshly ground black pepper

1 ciabatta loaf, cut into 4 portions, or

4 ciabatta rolls

4 tablespoons (60 g) pesto

4 ounces (115 g) crumbled feta cheese

8 oil-packed sun-dried tomatoes, thinly sliced

4 fresh basil leaves, roughly torn

Grilled Salmon Sandwiches with BBQ Rémoulade

▶ **Yield:** 4 panini

2 tablespoons (28 ml) extra-virgin olive oil

8 slices of sourdough bread, sliced from a dense bakery loaf

1 skin-on salmon fillet (1 pound, or 455 g)

Coarse salt and freshly ground black pepper

1 recipe BBQ Rémoulade (recipe follows)

½ cup (10 g) baby arugula

8 thin slices of red onion, separated into rings

2 plum tomatoes (such as Roma), thinly sliced and seeded

This is a darn good grilled fish sandwich. Sorry, I know that's not overly descriptive, but those are the words that run through my head every time I bite into one. It's what you get when you take a fresh, flavorful fish like salmon, grill it to perfection in minutes on the panini press, dress it in a creamy-tangy, barbecue sauce–spiked rémoulade sauce, and layer it in with tomatoes, onions, and arugula on crunchy grilled bread.

1. Heat the panini press to medium-high heat. If your panini press comes with a removable drip tray, make sure it is in place (see page 12).

2. Brush 1 tablespoon (15 ml) olive oil over one side of all the bread slices to flavor the outside of the sandwiches. In batches, grill the bread until it's toasted, 2 to 3 minutes.

3. Divide the salmon into four equal portions. Rub the remaining 1 tablespoon (15 ml) olive oil over the salmon, season it with salt and pepper, and transfer it, skin side down, to the grill. Close the lid and grill the salmon until it's cooked through, 5 to 7 minutes. Remove the salmon skin.

4. *For each sandwich:* Lay two slices of grilled bread on a cutting board, oiled-sides down. Spread some BBQ Rémoulade on each. On one slice, pile a small bed of arugula, some red onion rings, a portion of salmon, and a few slices of tomato. Close the sandwich with the other slice of bread.

BBQ Rémoulade

Yield: About $3/4$ cup (175 g)

Rémoulade starts out similar to tartar sauce, but cooks often add different spices and ingredients that make it its own distinct sauce. I've given this rémoulade a smoky barbecue spin that not only tastes great with salmon, but also makes a great dip for vegetables or shrimp, or even a steak condiment.

½ cup (115 g) mayonnaise
¼ cup (65 g) barbecue sauce
1 scallion, chopped
2 tablespoons (8 g) chopped fresh parsley
2 tablespoons (15 g) minced celery
1 garlic clove, minced
Coarse salt and freshly ground black pepper

In a small bowl, whisk together the mayonnaise, barbecue sauce, scallion, parsley, celery, and garlic and season with salt and pepper to taste. Cover the bowl and refrigerate the Rémoulade until you're ready to use it.

Grilled Salmon BLT Panini

▶ **Yield:** 4 panini

½ cup (115 g) mayonnaise
2 tablespoons (30 g) pesto
(see Note)
2 tablespoons (28 ml)
extra-virgin olive oil
8 slices sourdough bread,
sliced from a dense
bakery loaf
1 skin-on salmon fillet
(1 pound, 455 g)
Coarse salt and freshly
ground black pepper
½ cup (10 g) baby arugula
8 strips of cooked bacon
2 plum tomatoes (such as
Roma), thinly sliced and
seeded

Could the BLT be the best sandwich invention ever? Someone somewhere along the line figured out that three simple key ingredients—bacon, lettuce, and tomato—form a trifecta that is not only perfect as a stand-alone sandwich but also sets the foundation for so many others. You can add almost anything—including salmon—to a BLT and it will still taste amazing!

1. In a small bowl, whisk together the mayonnaise and pesto until well combined. Cover the bowl and put it in the refrigerator until you're ready to assemble the panini.

2. Heat the panini press to medium-high heat. If your panini press comes with a removable drip tray, make sure it is in place (see page 12).

3. Brush 1 tablespoon (15 ml) olive oil over one side of all the bread slices to flavor the outside of the sandwiches. In batches, grill the bread until it's toasted, 2 to 3 minutes.

4. Divide the salmon into four equal portions. Rub the remaining 1 tablespoon (15 ml) olive oil over the salmon, season it with salt and pepper, and transfer it, skin side down, to the grill. Close the lid and grill the salmon until it's cooked through, 5 to 7 minutes. Remove the salmon skin.

5. *For each sandwich:* Lay two slices of grilled bread on a cutting board, oiled-sides down. Spread some pesto mayonnaise on each. On one slice, pile a small bed of arugula, a portion of salmon, 2 bacon strips, and a few slices of tomato. Close the sandwich with the other slice of bread.

NOTE: Alternatively, if you don't have pesto on hand, you can mix up a quick batch of Basil-Garlic Mayonnaise (page 35).

Tuna Melt Panini

▶ **Yield:** 4 panini

TUNA SALAD
2 cans (5 ounce, or 140 g each) solid white albacore tuna packed in water, drained

1 celery rib, minced

2 tablespoons (28 ml) mayonnaise

Coarse salt and freshly ground black pepper

PANINI
4 tablespoons (½ stick, or 55 g) butter, at room temperature

8 slices of sourdough, rye, or other rustic bread, sliced from a dense bakery loaf

8 thin slices red onion, separated into rings

2 plum tomatoes (such as Roma)

4 ounces (115 g) sharp cheddar or Swiss cheese, sliced

Sandwiches made with a salad of canned tuna, mayonnaise, and celery were "tunafish" to me growing up because that's what my parents, both New Yorkers, called them. But I've rarely, if ever, heard the word in California, where I've lived for most of my life. It's always "tuna salad" or "tuna sandwich"—never "tunafish." I'm thinking it might be a regional term, like "pocketbook," "dungarees," and "AHHranges"—other notables from my early vocabulary that used to perplex my childhood friends on the West Coast.

Whatever you want to call it, few things beat a good old-fashioned, diner-style tuna melt, draped in cheese on toasty bread. I like my tuna/tunafish/tuna salad very simple, with just mayonnaise and celery, but if there are other ingredients you prefer to add in, go right ahead—the more the merrier!

1. In a medium-size bowl, mix the tuna, celery, and mayonnaise until well combined. Season the tuna salad with salt and pepper to taste.

2. Heat the panini press to medium-high heat.

3. *For each sandwich:* Spread butter on two slices of bread to flavor the outside of the sandwich. Flip over one slice of bread and top it with tuna salad, red onions, tomatoes, and cheese. Close the sandwich with the other slice of bread, buttered side up.

4. Grill two panini at a time, with the lid closed, until the cheese is melted and the bread is toasted, 4 to 5 minutes.

Pan Bagnat Panini (French-Style Tuna Melt)

▶ **Yield:** 4 panini

The *pan bagnat* (pahn bahn-YAH) sandwich from France gets its name, which translates to "bathed bread," from the boldly flavored fillings that seep into the crusty baguette. I've taken the traditional ingredients—tuna, olives, green bell peppers, red onions, and tomatoes—and added some zesty marinated mozzarella to create a tuna melt–style panini version of this French classic.

1. *Marinated Mozzarella:* Combine the olive oil, garlic, basil, oregano, thyme, and red pepper flakes in a medium-size bowl. Add the mozzarella and toss the cheese in the marinade to coat it well. Let the cheese marinate for 1 hour at room temperature to allow the flavors to seep in.

2. Heat the panini press to medium-high heat.

3. *For each sandwich:* Slice off the domed top of a baguette portion to create a flat grilling surface. Split the baguette to create top and bottom halves. Spread 1 tablespoon (8 g) olive tapenade inside the bottom half of the baguette. Top the tapenade with green bell peppers, tuna, red onions, tomatoes, and Marinated Mozzarella. Close the sandwich with the top baguette half.

4. Grill two panini at a time, with the lid closed, until the cheese is melted and the baguettes are toasted, 5 to 6 minutes.

MARINATED MOZZARELLA
- 2 tablespoons (28 ml) extra-virgin olive oil
- 1 garlic clove, minced
- ¼ teaspoon dried basil
- ¼ teaspoon dried oregano
- ¼ teaspoon dried thyme
- A pinch of red pepper flakes
- 4 ounces (115 g) fresh mozzarella cheese, sliced

PANINI
- 1 French baguette, cut into 4 portions, or 4 mini baguettes
- 4 tablespoons (32 g) olive tapenade
- ½ medium-size green bell pepper, thinly sliced
- 2 cans (5 ounce, or 140 g) solid white albacore tuna packed in oil, drained and flaked
- ½ small red onion, sliced
- 2 plum tomatoes (such as Roma), thinly sliced and seeded

Tuna and White Bean–Chive Hummus Tartines

▶ **Yield:** 4 tartines

I think of these tartines (open-faced sandwiches) as lighter versions of a tuna melt. You still have the star ingredient—tuna salad—but it's tossed in red wine vinegar and olive oil rather than mayonnaise. Instead of cheese, the white bean–chive hummus brings a creamy texture to the sandwich as well as lots of fresh flavor. For even more flavor, as well as a bit of crunch, I like to use olive bread for these tartines. You can serve these as open-faced tartines or grill more bread to close the sandwiches.

1. Toss the tuna with 1 tablespoon (15 ml) of the olive oil and the vinegar in a medium-size bowl. Season the tuna with salt and pepper to taste.

2. Heat the panini press to high heat.

3. Brush the remaining 1 tablespoon (15 ml) olive oil on each slice of olive bread. Grill the bread, with the lid closed, until it's toasted and golden grill marks appear, about 2 minutes.

4. Spread 2 tablespoons (30 g) of White Bean–Chive Hummus on each slice of grilled bread. Top the hummus with red onions, tomato slices, tuna, and chopped basil.

(continued on next page)

2 cans (5 ounce, or 140 g each) solid white albacore tuna packed in water, drained and flaked

2 tablespoons (28 ml) extra-virgin olive oil

1 tablespoon (15 ml) red wine vinegar

Coarse salt and freshly ground black pepper

4 slices olive bread, sliced from a dense bakery loaf

½ cup (120 g) White Bean-Chive Hummus (recipe follows)

½ small red onion, sliced

2 plum tomatoes (such as Roma)

2 tablespoons (5 g) chopped fresh basil

Tuna and White Bean–Chive Hummus
Tartines *(continued)*

White Bean–Chive Hummus

▶ **Yield:** About 1¹/₂ cups (360 g)

A favorite pastime of my youngest sister when were growing up was to grab a handful of the chives that my mom grew in our backyard, eat them, and then come running up to my middle sister and me, breathing a loud "HHHHHHiiiiiiii!!" in our direction. Despite that rather fragrant introduction to chives, I'm still a big fan of them—for both their gentle oniony flavor and the fact that they look like green herb sprinkles when you chop them. When I was considering how to bring bright, herbal flavors to plain white bean hummus, chives and parsley both jumped to mind. That pale green hue lets you know right away that you're in for something fresh tasting.

You can use hummus as a healthy substitute for ingredients like cheese or mayonnaise on your panini, or just serve it as a dip for pita chips and raw veggies.

1 can (15 ounces, or 425 g) cannellini beans, rinsed and drained
2 tablespoons (30 g) tahini
2 tablespoons (28 ml) freshly squeezed lemon juice
1 garlic clove, peeled
2 tablespoons (6 g) chopped fresh chives
2 tablespoons (8 g) chopped fresh parsley
¹/₄ teaspoon ground cumin
¹/₄ teaspoon coarse salt
A pinch of cayenne pepper

Combine all of the ingredients in a food processor and process until the mixture is smooth. Serve the hummus immediately or cover and refrigerate until you're ready to use it.

Bacon Crab Melt Panini

▶ **Yield:** 4 panini

This is the type of sandwich that, to me, falls under the category of "diner food." And I say that as someone who has a high respect for diners and their iconic place in American culture. Let's be honest: Some of the ingredients they use aren't always the healthiest—but, man, the food sure tastes good.

If I ever encountered Bacon Crab Melt Panini on a diner menu—or any menu, really—it's a safe bet that I'd order it. The sandwich starts with crabmeat that's tossed in a dressing with tons of bright, fresh flavors, and then layered onto sourdough bread with sliced tomato, bacon, and sharp cheddar cheese. And then, of course, it gets all toasty and melty on the grill. I'm not ashamed to admit that I like to indulge in such things from time to time. Somehow I have a feeling I'm not the only one!

1. Heat the panini press to medium-high heat.

2. In a medium-size bowl, combine the mayonnaise, celery, lemon juice, Old Bay seasoning, Dijon mustard, and salt and pepper to taste. Stir in the drained crabmeat.

3. *For each sandwich:* Spread butter on two slices of bread to flavor the outside of the sandwich. Flip over one slice and top the other side with cheese, crab salad, bacon, tomatoes, and more cheese. Close the sandwich with the other slice of bread, buttered side up.

4. Grill two panini at a time, with the lid closed, until the cheese is melted and the bread is toasted, 4 to 5 minutes.

4 tablespoons (60 g) mayonnaise

2 tablespoons (13 g) chopped celery

1 tablespoon (15 ml) freshly squeezed lemon juice

½ teaspoon Old Bay Seasoning

½ teaspoon Dijon mustard

Coarse salt and freshly ground black pepper

12 ounces (340 g) lump crabmeat, drained well

4 tablespoons (½ stick, or 55 g) butter, at room temperature

8 slices of sourdough or other rustic white bread, sliced from a dense bakery loaf

4 ounces (115 g) sharp cheddar cheese, sliced

8 strips of cooked bacon

2 plum tomatoes (such as Roma), thinly sliced and seeded

Smoked Salmon, Goat Cheese, and Fennel Slaw Panini

▶ **Yield:** 4 panini

4 bagels (plain, sesame, poppy seed, or everything are all good choices)

4 ounces (115 g) goat cheese, at room temperature, sliced into medallions

1 recipe Fennel Slaw (page 87)

4 ounces (115 g) smoked salmon

Smoked salmon—preferably on a sesame bagel—is my husband's favorite food in the whole world. On those few occasions throughout the year when he treats himself to some, it turns into a bit of a production. He gathers all of the necessary items within easy reach—a small plate, a butter knife, his just-toasted bagels, a tub of whipped cream cheese, and, of course, his sleeve of salmon. Then he takes his place at the kitchen table and digs in. He doesn't say much as he repeatedly assembles "the perfect bite" with just the right ratio of salmon to cream cheese, but when I glance over at him, the look on his face lets me know that he's one contented man.

1. Heat the panini press to medium-high heat.

2. *For each sandwich:* Cut a sliver off the rounded top surface of a bagel to create a flat grilling surface. Split the bagel to create top and bottom halves. Spread a layer of goat cheese on the bottom half and then top it with Fennel Slaw and smoked salmon. Close the sandwich with the top bagel half.

3. Grill two panini at a time, with the lid closed, until the goat cheese is softened and the bagels are toasted, 4 to 6 minutes.

Smoked Trout, Boursin, and Cucumber Panini

▶ **Yield:** 4 panini

Admittedly, smoked salmon and smoked trout look and taste a whole lot alike (the two fish are closely related), but for some reason it feels as though I'm eating something a little more exotic when I go for the trout. Maybe it just seems special because I don't see it quite as often in stores or on menus. Here, I've paired smoked trout with Boursin—a creamy cheese that comes in a variety of flavors—for a slightly different spin on the smoked salmon and cream cheese combination we've all enjoyed forever.

1. Heat the panini press to medium-high heat.

2. *For each sandwich:* Spread butter on two slices of bread to flavor the outside of the sandwich. Flip over both slices of bread and spread Boursin on the other side of each slice. Top one slice with smoked trout and cucumbers. Close the sandwich with the other slice of bread, buttered side up.

3. Grill two panini at a time, with the lid closed, until the bread is toasted, about 3 minutes.

NOTE: You can find Boursin near the cream cheese in the refrigerated section of most grocery stores. I particularly like the Garlic and Fine Herbs flavor for this recipe.

4 tablespoons (½ stick, or 55 g) butter, at room temperature

8 slices of whole-grain bread, sliced from a dense bakery loaf

1 package (5.2 ounces, or 145 g) Boursin cheese (see Note)

4 ounces (115 g) smoked trout fillets, skin removed

½ cucumber, peeled and thinly sliced

Grilled Shrimp Tostadas with Mashed Black Beans and Avocado Salsa Fresca

▶ **Yield:** 4 tostadas

SHRIMP

2 tablespoons (28 ml)
   vegetable oil
1 teaspoon freshly
   squeezed lime juice
1 teaspoon chili powder
¼ teaspoon ground cumin
¼ teaspoon coarse salt
1 pound (455 g) raw large
   shrimp, peeled and
   deveined

MASHED BLACK BEANS

2 tablespoons (28 ml)
   vegetable oil
3 garlic cloves, minced
1 can (15 ounce, or 425 g)
   of black beans, rinsed
   and drained
1 to 2 tablespoons (15 to
   28 ml) water
Coarse salt

TOSTADAS

1 tablespoon (15 ml)
   vegetable oil
4 (8 inches, or 20 cm each)
   flour tortillas
Coarse salt
4 ounces (115 g) crumbled
   queso fresco or shredded
   Monterey Jack (about 1
   cup)
1 cup Avocado Salsa Fresca
   (page 111)

You can grill half a pound (225 g) of shrimp on the panini press in about 2 minutes. That is reason enough to have panini-grilled shrimp in your regular weeknight dinner rotation, don't you think?

For these tostadas, I first let the shrimp bathe in a chili-lime marinade before they hit the grill. Also grilled on the panini press: the tostada shells. You just brush a little oil on regular tortillas and after a minute or so on the grill they're toasty, crisp, and ready for toppings. Black beans mashed with garlic (a terrific technique I learned from a Rick Bayless recipe) and sprinkled with *queso fresco* make a flavorful base to hold the shrimp on the tostada, and an Avocado Salsa Fresca brings a punch of bright, Southwestern flavor to the dish.

1. *Shrimp:* In a medium-size bowl, stir together the vegetable oil, lime juice, chili powder, cumin, and salt. Add the shrimp and toss to coat them in the marinade. Cover the bowl and let the shrimp marinate in the refrigerator while you prepare the rest of the dish. (Note: The citric acid in the lime juice can start to "cook" the shrimp after a while, so I don't recommend marinating the shrimp for longer than 30 minutes.)

2. *Mashed Black Beans:* Heat the vegetable oil in a large skillet over medium heat. Add the garlic and stir it in the oil until it's fragrant and just beginning to brown, about 1 minute. Add the black beans. Give the beans a rough mash with a potato masher (they should still be a bit chunky) and cook them for another minute or two until they're heated through. Take the pan off the heat and stir in 1 to 2 tablespoons (15 to 28 ml) of water, until the beans are spreadable. Season the beans with coarse salt to taste and partially cover the pan to keep them warm.

3. *Tostadas:* Heat the panini press to medium-high heat.

4. Lightly brush a tortilla with vegetable oil and transfer it to the grill. Sprinkle the tortilla with a little salt and close the lid. Grill the tortilla until it's crisped and golden grill marks appear, 1 to 2 minutes. Repeat with the rest of the tortillas. Keep the grill heated.

5. Remove the shrimp from the marinade (discard the remaining marinade) and put half of them on the grill. Close the lid and grill the shrimp until they're cooked through and opaque, about 2 minutes. Repeat with the remaining shrimp.

6. Spread some Mashed Black Beans over each grilled tortilla (if the beans have cooled off too much to be spreadable, put them back on the stove over low heat for a few minutes and stir in water, 1 teaspoon at a time). Top them with *queso fresco*, grilled shrimp, and Avocado Salsa Fresca and serve.

Avocado Salsa Fresca

▶ **Yield:** About 2 ½ cups (575 g)

Mix up this fresh and easy avocado salsa and set it in the refrigerator; by the time you're done preparing the tostadas, the flavors will have had a chance to blend together just right. Scoop up any leftover salsa with tortilla chips or use it to top tacos, fish, or crostini.

> 1 medium-size ripe avocado, pitted, peeled, and diced
> 2 medium-size ripe tomatoes, diced
> 3 tablespoons (30 g) chopped red onion
> ½ of a jalapeño pepper, seeded and finely chopped
> 2 tablespoons (2 g) chopped fresh cilantro
> 1 tablespoon (15 ml) freshly squeezed lime juice
> ¼ teaspoon coarse salt

Toss all of the ingredients together in a medium-size bowl. Cover the bowl and refrigerate for 30 minutes to allow the flavors to combine. The salsa is best the day it's made, but it will stay fresh in the refrigerator for up to 2 days.

Seared Ahi and Avocado Salad

▶ **Yield:** 4 servings

TUNA

1 tablespoon (15 ml) extra-virgin olive oil

1 sashimi-grade ahi tuna steak (1 pound, or 455 g), about 1 inch (2.5 cm) thick

Coarse salt and freshly ground black pepper

SALAD

1 head butter lettuce, torn into large pieces

¼ red onion, thinly sliced

½ cup (90 g) sliced roasted red bell peppers

½ cup (78 g) shelled cooked edamame, thawed if frozen

1 recipe Ginger Vinaigrette (recipe follows)

1 medium-size ripe avocado, pitted, peeled, and sliced

One of my best friends doesn't consider herself to be much of a cook, but she knows good, healthy food when she eats it. The queen of our local takeout scene, she is fully prepared for any last-minute ordering, with all of the restaurants programmed into her cell phone. A favorite order of hers is a seared ahi salad that's been tossed in ginger vinaigrette with goodies like avocado, edamame, roasted red bell peppers, and greens. I ventured to make my own version at home—searing the ahi to perfection on the panini press for a mere 90 seconds—and was won over by this fabulous Cal-Asian salad combination as well.

1. *Tuna:* Heat the panini press to high heat. If your panini press comes with a removable drip tray, make sure it is in place (see page 12).

2. Brush the olive oil over both sides of the tuna and season the tuna with salt and pepper.

3. Grill the tuna, with the lid closed, until it's seared on the outside but still bright red on the inside, about 90 seconds. Transfer the fish to a cutting board and slice it thinly across the grain.

4. *Salad:* Toss the lettuce, red onion, roasted red peppers, edamame, and 2 tablespoons (28 ml) of the Ginger Vinaigrette together in a large bowl.

5. Divide the salad among four plates. Arrange slices of tuna and avocado on top of each salad and drizzle more Ginger Vinaigrette over the top (you probably will have extra dressing for later use).

Ginger Vinaigrette

▶ **Yield:** About ¾ cup (175 ml)

When it comes to salad dressings, I'm a vinaigrette girl all the way. Once you've got the classic ratio down—3 parts oil, 1 part vinegar or other acid—you can customize vinaigrettes to fit any flavor profile. For Asian-inspired salads, a ginger-based dressing is a perfect complement.

1 tablespoon (15 ml) reduced-sodium soy sauce
1 tablespoon (15 ml) freshly squeezed lemon juice
1 tablespoon (15 ml) plus 2 teaspoons (10 ml) rice wine vinegar
2 garlic cloves, minced
2 teaspoons grated fresh ginger
1 teaspoon honey
½ teaspoon Dijon mustard
½ teaspoon sugar
½ cup (120 ml) extra-virgin olive oil
Freshly ground black pepper

In a small bowl, whisk together the soy sauce, lemon juice, vinegar, garlic, ginger, honey, mustard, and sugar. Gradually whisk in the olive oil. Season the vinaigrette with black pepper to taste. Store any leftovers in an airtight container in the refrigerator for up to 4 days.

Grilled Fish Tacos

▶ **Yield:** 4 servings

FISH
¼ cup (60 ml) vegetable oil
2 tablespoons (28 ml) freshly squeezed lime juice
2 teaspoons ancho chili powder
¼ teaspoon coarse salt
1 flaky white fish fillet (1 pound, or 455 g), such as mahi mahi or halibut

ACCOMPANIMENTS
8 (8 inches, or 20 cm each) corn or flour tortillas, warmed
Shredded cabbage
Hot sauce or salsa
Sliced red onions
Sliced scallions
Chipotle Sour Cream (recipe follows)
Chopped fresh cilantro
Lime wedges

When out-of-town friends come to visit us in San Diego, the one local delicacy they always want to try is fish tacos. They first became popular down in Baja California and, thankfully, found their way north of the border.

Grilling the fish on the panini press takes a matter of minutes and it comes out moist, flaky, and flavorful. I add some spicy chipotles to the traditional sour cream sauce to boost the overall flavor even further.

1. *Fish:* Whisk together the oil, lime juice, ancho chile powder, and salt in a shallow glass dish. Add the fish and turn to coat it in the marinade. Cover the dish and let the fish marinate in the refrigerator for 20 minutes.

2. Heat the panini press to medium-high heat. If your panini press comes with a removable drip tray, make sure it is in place (see page 12).

3. Transfer the fish to the grill and close the lid so that the upper plate is resting on the fish without pressing it. Grill the fish until it's cooked through, 3 to 4 minutes. With a spatula, carefully transfer the fish to a plate.

4. Divide the fish among the tortillas (it should flake easily) and top each taco with cabbage, salsa, red onions, scallions, and a dollop of Chipotle Sour Cream. Garnish with a little chopped cilantro and serve with lime wedges.

¼ cup (60 g) sour cream
¼ cup (60 g) mayonnaise
3 tablespoons (45 ml) freshly squeezed lime juice
1 chipotle in adobo sauce, minced

Chipotle Sour Cream

▶ **Yield:** About ¾ cup (175 g)

In a small bowl, whisk together the sour cream, mayonnaise, lime juice, and chipotle. Cover the bowl and refrigerate the mixture until you're ready to use it. It will stay fresh in the refrigerator for about 3 days.

NATURE'S BOUNTY

Fruit, Vegetables, and Beans on the Panini Press

Roasted Apples, Brie, and Pecan Panini

▶ **Yield:** 4 panini

The idea for combining roasted apples and Brie in a sandwich came from a PaniniHappy.com reader from Vancouver. At the time that I first posted this recipe on the blog, I had never tried roasted apples before. I immediately fell in love with the caramelized crust that forms on the bottom from the sugars in the apple. In keeping with these homey, autumnal flavors, I added crunchy pecans for some nutty texture and grilled it all on cinnamon raisin bread.

1. Heat the oven or toaster oven to 400°F (200°C, or gas mark 6).

2. Spray a baking sheet with nonstick cooking spray and arrange the apples on the sheet. Roast the apples until they are soft and golden brown, with a caramelized crust on the bottom, 15 to 20 minutes.

3. Heat the panini press to medium-high heat.

4. *For each sandwich:* Spread butter on two slices of bread to flavor the outside of the sandwich. Flip over one slice and top the other side with Brie, roasted apple slices, and pecans. Close the sandwich with the other slice of bread, buttered-side up.

5. Grill two panini at a time, with the lid closed, until the cheese is melted and the bread is toasted, 4 to 5 minutes.

1 medium-size apple, cored and cut into ¼-inch (6 mm) thick slices

4 tablespoons (½ stick, or 55 g) butter, at room temperature

8 slices of cinnamon raisin bread, sliced from a dense bakery loaf

4 ounces (115 g) Brie cheese (with or without the rind), sliced

¼ cup (28 g) chopped pecans

Grilled Asparagus Tartines with Fresh Ricotta, Pesto, and Scallions

▶ **Yield:** 4 tartines

1 pound (455 g) asparagus, trimmed to the length of a ciabatta slice
2 tablespoons (28 ml) extra-virgin olive oil
Coarse salt and freshly ground black pepper
4 slices ciabatta or other crusty rustic bread
4 tablespoons (65 g) pesto
½ cup (125 g) ricotta cheese
1 scallion, chopped

I first made these tartines in celebration of St. Patrick's Day—not that they're especially Irish, but they sure are green. With grilled asparagus, scallions, and basil pesto, they're packed with fresh, springtime flavor, and they come together in minutes. You can easily scale down these open-faced sandwiches to crostini size, using rounds of baguette, and serve them as appetizers.

1. Heat the panini press to medium-high heat.

2. In a large bowl, toss the asparagus with 2 teaspoons of the olive oil and season with salt and pepper. Grill the asparagus, with the lid closed, until they're tender and grill marks appear, 3 to 4 minutes.

3. Brush another 2 teaspoons of the olive oil over the ciabatta slices and grill the bread, with the lid closed, until it's toasted and grill marks appear, 2 to 3 minutes.

4. Spread 1 tablespoon (15 g) pesto on each slice of ciabatta. Spoon on a few tablespoons (47 to 65 g) of ricotta and top it with grilled asparagus (you'll have extra asparagus—you can save it to enjoy on its own, add it to a salad or pasta, or just make more tartines!) and a sprinkling of chopped scallions. Finish the tartines by drizzling the remaining 2 teaspoons olive oil over the top and grinding on a little more black pepper.

Grilled Portobello Cheese Steak Panini

▶ **Yield:** 4 panini

For the non-meat-eaters in your life, try these panini. Meaty marinated portobello mushroom caps replace the traditional steak, but I swear you'll hardly notice.

1. Heat the panini press to medium-high heat.

2. Brush oil on both sides of the onion slices and season them with salt and pepper. Grill the onions until they're tender and dark grill marks appear, 6 to 8 minutes. Separate the onion rounds into rings.

3. *For each sandwich:* Split a ciabatta portion to create top and bottom halves. Pile some of the grilled onion rings inside the bottom half. Top the onions with sliced mushrooms, hot peppers, and cheese. Close the sandwich with the top ciabatta half.

4. Grill two panini at a time, with the lid closed, until the cheese is melted and the ciabatta is toasted, 5 to 6 minutes.

1 tablespoon (15 ml) vegetable oil

1 medium-size onion, sliced into ½-inch (1.3 cm) thick rounds (rings intact)

1 ciabatta loaf, cut into 4 portions, or 4 ciabatta rolls

4 Marinated Portobello Mushrooms (see below), cut into strips

4 jarred hot Italian peppers, such as banana peppers or fried "longhot" cayenne peppers, sliced

4 ounces (115 g) sharp provolone cheese, sliced

Marinated Portobello Mushrooms

▶ **Yield:** 4 servings

Make It Ahead: You can marinate and grill your mushrooms ahead of time—they'll keep for 3 to 5 days in a covered container in the fridge.

1. Wipe any dirt from the mushroom caps with a damp paper towel. Pop out the stems and scoop out the gills with a spoon; discard the stems and gills.

2. Combine the olive oil, vinegar, garlic, thyme, mustard, salt, and pepper in a shallow bowl. Add the mushroom caps and roll them around in the marinade a bit to coat them. Let the mushrooms marinate at room temperature, turning them occasionally, for 30 minutes.

3. Heat the panini press to medium-high heat. If your panini press comes with a removable drip tray, make sure it is in place (see page 12).

4. Remove the mushrooms from the marinade, transfer them to the grill, and close the lid. Grill until they're tender and dark grill marks appear, about 5 minutes.

4 portobello mushrooms
¼ cup extra-virgin olive oil
¼ cup balsamic vinegar
2 garlic cloves, minced
1 teaspoon dried thyme
1 teaspoon Dijon mustard
½ teaspoon coarse salt
¼ teaspoon freshly ground black pepper

Burrata Caprese Tartines

▶ **Yield:** 4 tartines

I fell in love with burrata cheese the very first time I tried it. My knife broke through the outer mozzarella shell of the little white ball of cheese and released the cream and mozzarella on the inside. With a sprinkle of salt and a splash of olive oil on top, it was simply divine. Here, I've added burrata to summery caprese-style open-faced sandwiches with grilled fresh tomatoes, basil pesto, and crunchy roasted pistachios.
It's easier to find burrata on restaurant menus than in stores, but I seek it out in specialty cheese shops. Water-packed fresh mozzarella is a good alternative if burrata isn't available near you.

1. Heat the panini press to high heat.

2. Brush 1 tablespoon olive oil on the bread slices and grill them, with the lid closed, until they're toasted, about 2 minutes.

3. Drizzle another tablespoon of olive oil over the cut sides of the tomatoes and season them with salt and pepper. Place the tomatoes, cut sides down, on the grill, close the lid, and grill them until they're tender and wrinkly and caramelized on the bottom, 8 to 10 minutes.

4. Spread a layer of pesto on each slice of grilled bread. Top the pesto with grilled tomatoes, a portion of burrata, and a scattering of pistachios. Drizzle a little olive oil over the top and season the tartines with salt and pepper to taste.

4 slices Italian, sourdough, or other
rustic white bread, sliced from a dense bakery loaf
2 tablespoons extra-virgin olive oil, plus more for garnish
4 plum tomatoes (such as Roma), halved lengthwise
Coarse salt and freshly ground black pepper
4 tablespoons pesto, purchased or homemade (page 101)
1 (4-ounce) ball burrata cheese, cut into
4 portions
¼ cup roasted, salted shelled pistachios

Kale, Grill-Roasted Garlic, and Cheddar Panini

▶ **Yield:** 4 panini

SAUTÉED KALE
1 tablespoon (15 ml) extra-virgin olive oil
1 shallot, thinly sliced
⅛ teaspoon red pepper flakes
1 pound (455 g) kale, stems removed and leaves roughly chopped
½ cup (120 ml) water
1 tablespoon (15 ml) apple cider vinegar
Coarse salt

PANINI
4 tablespoons (½ stick, or 55 g) butter, at room temperature
8 slices of rustic white bread, sliced from a dense bakery loaf
1 recipe Grill-Roasted Garlic (recipe follows)
4 ounces (115 g) sharp cheddar cheese, sliced

People have gone crazy for kale. It's full of nutrients and health benefits and you can add the flavorful greens to so many dishes—yes, even panini! The slight bitterness of sautéed kale is a wonderful counterpoint to tangy sharp cheddar cheese and sweet grill-roasted garlic.

Save any extra sautéed kale to enjoy as a side dish—it's fantastic on its own. It will keep for up to 5 days in a covered container in the refrigerator.

1. *Sautéed Kale:* Heat the olive oil in a large pot or Dutch oven over medium-high heat. Add the shallot and cook, stirring, until tender and fragrant, about 1 minute. Add the red pepper flakes and the kale and carefully toss the kale to coat it in the oil. Pour in the water. Cover the pot, reduce the heat to medium-low, and cook the kale until it's wilted and tender, another 10 minutes. Remove the pot from the heat, stir in the vinegar, and season the kale with salt to taste.

2. *For each sandwich:* Spread butter on two slices of bread to flavor the outside of the sandwich. Flip over one slice of bread and spread about a tablespoon (15 g) of soft garlic on the other side. Top the garlic with Sautéed Kale and cheese. Close the sandwich with the other slice of bread, buttered side up.

3. Grill two panini at a time, with the lid closed, until the cheese is melted and the bread is toasted, 4 to 5 minutes.

Grill-Roasted Garlic

▶ **Yield:** 1 head of garlic

I roast the garlic right on the panini press—it takes less time than the oven and, especially in summer, I'm glad don't have to heat up the house. Besides using grill-roasted garlic as a flavorful spread for panini, you can also puree it for sauces and dips, add it as a pizza or pasta topping, or even just eat the sweet cloves on their own. It's the recipe that keeps on giving!

1 head of garlic
2 teaspoons extra-virgin olive oil
A pinch of coarse salt

1. Heat the panini press to medium-high heat.

2. Peel away the papery outer skin from the head of garlic, keeping the head intact. Slice off ¼ inch (6 mm) from the top of the garlic head, exposing the cloves. Lay the garlic head on a piece of aluminum foil large enough to wrap it. Drizzle the cut side with olive oil and season it with salt. Wrap the garlic in the foil and place it, cut side down, on the grill. Close the lid and grill the garlic until the cloves are very soft and tender, about 30 minutes. Once they're cool enough to touch, squeeze the roasted garlic cloves out of their skins. You can freeze any leftover whole cloves on a baking sheet and then transfer them to a zipper-top plastic bag or covered container.

Mediterranean Grilled Vegetable Tartines

▶ **Yield:** 4 tartines

1 tablespoon (15 ml)
  extra-virgin olive oil
4 slices rustic white bread,
  sliced from a dense
  bakery loaf
½ cup (120 g) White Bean–
  Chive Hummus (page
  106)
½ recipe Grilled Herbed
  Vegetables
  (page 128)
4 ounces (115 g) crumbled
  feta cheese
Chopped chives, for garnish

Looking back, I've probably been making tartines (open-faced sandwiches with a French name) since I was a kid. I used to pile a bunch of ingredients I liked—salami, American cheese, and ketchup may or may not have been involved—on a slice of bread, heat it all up in the microwave, and enjoy. Ah, youth . . . .

These days marinated grilled vegetables, White Bean–Chive Hummus, and feta are more my style. It's a terrific assortment of Mediterranean flavors all set atop some crunchy grilled bread. Meat lovers: Don't let all the vegetables fool you—this healthy-yet-hearty sandwich definitely gives you something to sink your teeth into.

1. Heat the panini press to high heat.

2. Brush a little olive oil on one side of each slice of bread. Working in batches if necessary, transfer the bread slices, oiled sides up, to the grill, close the lid, and grill until they are toasted and grill marks appear, 2 to 3 minutes.

3. Spread 2 tablespoons (28 ml) White Bean-Chive Hummus on each slice of bread. Top the hummus with Grilled Herbed Vegetables and a sprinkling of feta and chives.

Grilled Acorn Squash with Cranberry-Ginger Maple Syrup and Toasted Walnuts

▶ **Yield:** *4 servings*

Grilling acorn squash on the panini press is much faster than roasting—this dish takes only 30 minutes, start to finish. Plus, I think the grill marks are kind of pretty, especially with the dark scalloped edges of the acorn squash. The cranberry-ginger maple syrup is sweet, fruity, and gingery all at the same time, and it dresses up the dish even enough to serve on your holiday table.

While it probably isn't harmful to eat the acorn squash peel, many people choose not to do so. Just cut away the flesh with your fork or go ahead and pick up the slices with your hands and eat 'em like melon—I won't judge!

1 acorn squash
2 tablespoons (28 g) butter, melted
½ cup (120 ml) pure maple syrup
¼ cup (130 g) dried cranberries
½ teaspoon grated fresh ginger or a pinch of ground ginger
¼ cup (30 g) toasted chopped walnuts

1. Heat the panini press to medium-high heat.

2. Slice the acorn squash in half lengthwise, scoop out the seeds, and then slice the squash into ½-inch (1.3 cm) thick scalloped crescent moons.

3. Working in batches as needed, brush melted butter onto one side of as many slices of squash as will fit on your grill. Place the squash on the grill, buttered sides down, and brush butter on the other side. Close the grill so that the lid rests on the squash without pressing it. Grill the squash until it is tender and dark grill marks appear, about 7 minutes. Transfer the squash to a serving platter and tent the plate with foil to keep the squash warm while you grill the remaining batches.

4. While the squash is grilling, bring the maple syrup, cranberries, and ginger to a boil in a saucepan over high heat. Turn down the heat to medium-low and let the syrup simmer for 2 to 3 minutes. Remove the syrup from the heat.

5. Drizzle the cranberry-ginger maple syrup over the squash and garnish with toasted walnuts before serving.

Grilled Peach Salad with Toasted Pecans, Blue Cheese, and Honey Balsamic Syrup

▶ **Yield:** 6 servings

½ cup (55 g) chopped pecans
½ cup (170 g) honey
¼ cup (60 ml) balsamic vinegar
¼ teaspoon dried thyme
⅛ teaspoon black pepper
A pinch of coarse salt
1 tablespoon (14 g) butter, melted
3 peaches, halved and pitted
5 ounces (140 g) baby arugula
2 ounces (55 g) blue cheese, crumbled

The only pregnancy craving I can remember having was for ripe, juicy, summer peaches. For my entire second trimester with my daughter, I was eating them by the crate. I've slowed my consumption since then, but peaches remain my all-time favorite fruit (with strawberries coming in a close second).

For this salad I caramelize fresh peaches on a searing-hot panini press, then arrange them over a bed of peppery baby arugula, and fill them with a few dabs (not too much!) of tangy, creamy, crumbled blue cheese and a smattering of toasted pecans. And at the end the peaches get a drizzle of honey balsamic syrup.

1. Heat the oven or toaster oven to 350°F (180°F, or gas mark 4). Spread the pecans on a baking sheet and toast in the oven until they are fragrant, 4 to 6 minutes. Set them aside to cool.

2. In a small saucepan, heat the honey, balsamic vinegar, thyme, black pepper, and salt over medium heat. Stir to dissolve the honey and bring the mixture to a boil. Reduce the heat to medium-low and simmer, stirring occasionally, until the mixture is slightly thickened and syrupy, about 10 minutes. Remove the pan from the heat and let the honey balsamic syrup cool a bit—it will continue to thicken as it cools.

3. Heat the panini press to high heat. If your panini press comes with a removable drip tray, make sure it is in place (see page 12).

4. Brush a little melted butter on the cut sides of the peaches. Place the peaches on the grill, cut sides down. Close the lid so that the upper plate is hovering just above the peaches, if possible, or touching them very lightly. Grill the peaches until they are softened and grill marks appear, 4 to 5 minutes.

5. Spread the arugula on a serving platter and top with the peaches, cut sides up. Fill the cavity of each peach half with toasted pecans and blue cheese and drizzle with honey balsamic syrup.

Grilled Herbed Vegetables

▶ **Yield:** 6 to 8 servings

¼ cup (60 ml) extra-virgin olive oil

2 tablespoons (28 ml) balsamic vinegar

2 tablespoons (3 g) dried parsley

2 tablespoons (4 g) dried basil

1 tablespoon (2 g) dried marjoram

1 teaspoon coarse salt

½ teaspoon freshly ground black pepper

6 garlic cloves, minced

2 Japanese eggplants, sliced lengthwise into ¼-inch (6 mm) thick strips

2 small zucchini, sliced lengthwise into ¼-inch (6 mm) thick strips

1 red bell pepper, cored, seeded, and sliced into ½-inch (1.3 cm) thick strips

1 yellow bell pepper, cored, seeded, and sliced into ½-inch (1.3 cm) thick strips

1 small red onion

When I grill vegetables I like to make a large batch and then I use them for days, as a side dish, in sandwiches and salads, over pasta—you name it. They'll stay fresh for several days in the refrigerator. These fresh eggplants, zucchini, bell peppers, and onions get a good drenching in balsamic vinegar, olive oil, and herbs for robust Mediterranean flavor.

1. In a large zipper-top plastic bag, combine the olive oil, vinegar, parsley, basil, marjoram, salt, pepper, and garlic. Place the eggplants, zucchini, and bell peppers in the bag (reserve the onion). Seal the bag, roll the vegetables around in the marinade to coat them, and let the vegetables marinate for 1 to 2 hours in the refrigerator.

2. Heat the panini press to medium-high heat. If your panini press comes with a removable drip tray, make sure it is in place (see page 12).

3. Remove the vegetables from the marinade and reserve 1 table-spoon (15 ml) of the marinade. Grill the vegetables in batches of the same type of vegetable (all of the eggplant together, all of the zucchini together, etc.), with the lid closed, until they are tender and grill marks appear, 4 to 6 minutes, depending on the type of vegetable. Arrange the vegetables on a serving platter as they come off the grill. Slice the red onion into ¼-inch (6 mm) thick rounds. Drizzle the reserved marinade over the onions and grill them, with the lid closed, until they are tender and grill marks appear, 4 to 6 minutes. Serve the vegetables immediately or at room temperature.

Grilled Cheese Panzanella Salad

▶ **Yield:** About 4 servings

Panzanella is a true summertime treat. Chunks of day-old bread tossed with just-off-the-vine tomatoes, fresh basil, olive oil, and vinegar make up this traditional Italian salad. The dressing and juices from the tomatoes soak in and flavor the dry bread, which is where the real magic happens.

I had an idea one day . . . why not turn those chunks of stale bread into mini grilled cheese sandwiches? Traditionally, there's no cheese in panzanella, but there's no denying that mozzarella pairs perfectly with tomatoes and basil. I say food is food, so let's have fun with it. And nothing says fun, at least in the sandwich world, like teeny-tiny grilled cheese sandwiches in a salad.

1. *Grilled Cheese Croutons:* Heat the panini press to medium-high heat.

2. Place half the cheese on each of two slices of bread. Close each sandwich with a second slice of bread.

3. Grill both panini, with the lid closed, until the cheese is melted and the bread is toasted, 3 to 4 minutes. Transfer the panini to a cutting board. Trim the crusts from the panini and cut each sandwich into 1-inch (2.5 cm) squares.

4. *Salad:* Place the tomatoes, sliced red onions, torn basil, and Grilled Cheese Croutons in a large salad bowl.

5. Toss the salad with enough of the dressing to moisten the croutons without drenching them. Allow the flavors to meld at room temperature for 30 minutes before serving the salad.

GRILLED CHEESE CROUTONS

- 4 slices day-old sourdough or other rustic white bread, sliced from a dense bakery loaf
- 2 ounces (about ½ cup, or 55 g) shredded mozzarella or other semi-firm cheese

SALAD

- 4 medium-size ripe tomatoes, cut into bite-size chunks
- ½ small red onion, thinly sliced
- ¼ cup (6 g) torn fresh basil leaves
- 1 recipe White Balsamic Vinaigrette (page 75)

Spinach-Feta Quinoa Cakes with Lemon-Dill Yogurt Sauce

▶ **Yield:** 4 servings (8 to 10 patties)

1 tablespoon (15 ml) extra-virgin olive oil

½ cup (80 g) finely chopped onion

2 garlic cloves, finely chopped

5 ounces (140 g) baby spinach, chopped

2 large eggs, beaten

1¼ cups (231 g) cooked quinoa

2 ounces (55 g) crumbled feta cheese

1 tablespoon (4 g) chopped fresh dill

¼ teaspoon grated lemon zest

¼ teaspoon freshly ground black pepper

½ cup (60 g) bread crumbs

1 recipe Lemon-Dill Yogurt Sauce (recipe follows)

We're meat-eaters in our house, but we don't mind a good veggie burger every now and then either—especially if it's got lots of great flavor. I like to make mine with quinoa. Often considered a grain, it's actually a seed.

These grilled quinoa cakes take on the zesty flavors of a classic Greek spanakopita. Spoon a little lemon-dill yogurt sauce over the top for a light, healthy lunch.

1. Heat the olive oil in a large skillet over medium heat. Add the onion and garlic and cook, stirring often, until softened, about 4 minutes. Add the spinach and cook, stirring often, until wilted, about 3 minutes. Transfer the mixture to a medium-size bowl.

2. Add the eggs, quinoa, feta, dill, lemon zest, and black pepper and mix well. Mix in the bread crumbs and let the mixture sit for a few minutes to allow the bread crumbs to absorb some of the moisture.

3. Heat the panini press to medium-high heat.

4. Form quinoa patties about 2½ (6.5 cm) inches in diameter and ½ inch (1.3 cm) thick. Place the patties on the grill, in batches if necessary, and close the lid. Grill the patties until they're cooked through and browned on the outside, 4 to 5 minutes. Serve warm with lemon-dill yogurt sauce.

½ cup (115 g) plain Greek yogurt, reduced fat or whole

2 tablespoons (12 g) finely chopped scallions

2 teaspoons freshly squeezed lemon juice

2 teaspoons chopped fresh dill

Coarse salt and freshly ground black pepper

Lemon-Dill Yogurt Sauce

▶ **Yield:** About ½ cup (115 g)

This cool, creamy sauce brightens up all kinds of dishes, from salmon to falafel to raw vegetables.

Whisk together the yogurt, scallions, lemon juice, and dill in a small bowl. Season to taste with salt and pepper. Cover and refrigerate the sauce for at least 30 minutes to allow the flavors to meld.

GOOEY GOODNESS

Grilled Cheese on the Panini Press

PANINI

Cheddar and Apple Butter Panini with Rosemary Candied Pecans

▶ **Yield:** 4 panini

I really like cheddar and apples together, and this time, I've brought fresh rosemary into the mix. Rosemary candied pecans, spiced with cayenne, add a sweet crunch and gentle heat to these cheddar and apple butter panini. I grill it all on buttered rosemary bread to bring in more of those subtle, woodsy rosemary notes.

It takes a little extra time to make the pecans, but it's well worth it—plus, you'll have an irresistible snack while you wait for the panini to grill.

butter

1. Heat the panini press to medium-high heat.

2. *For each sandwich:* Spread butter on two slices of bread to flavor the outside of the sandwich. Flip over one slice and top the other side with cheese and some Rosemary Candied Pecans. Flip over the other slice of bread and spread 1 tablespoon (17 g) apple butter on the other side. Place it, buttered side up, on top of the sandwich to close it.

3. Grill two panini at a time, with the lid closed, until the cheese is melted and the bread is toasted, 4 to 5 minutes.

(continued on next page)

- 4 tablespoons (½ stick, or 55 g) butter, at room temperature
- 8 slices rosemary bread or other rustic white bread, sliced from a dense bakery loaf
- 8 ounces (225 g) sharp cheddar cheese, sliced
- ¼ cup (20 g) Rosemary Candied Pecans (recipe follows)
- 4 tablespoons (68 g) apple

Cheddar and Apple Butter Panini with Rosemary Candied Pecans

(continued)

Rosemary Candied Pecans

▶ **Yield:** 1 cup (80 g)

Caution: These pecans are very addictive!

¼ cup (50 g) sugar
2 teaspoons chopped fresh rosemary
½ teaspoon coarse salt
⅛ teaspoon ground cayenne pepper
1 large egg white
1 tablespoon (15 ml) water
1 cup (110 g) chopped pecans

1. Heat the oven or toaster oven to 300°F (150°F, or gas mark 2). Line a baking sheet with foil and spray the foil with nonstick cooking spray. Place the sugar, rosemary, salt, and cayenne
in a zipper-top plastic bag. Seal the bag and shake it well to combine it all.

2. In a medium-size bowl, whisk together the egg white and water until the mixture is slightly foamy. Add the pecans and toss to coat them well. With a slotted spoon, transfer the pecans to the bag with the sugar mixture. Seal the bag and shake it well to coat all of the pecans.

3. Transfer the coated pecans to the baking sheet and bake them for 30 minutes, giving them a stir with a fork after about 15 minutes. Set them aside to cool. The pecans should stay fresh in an airtight container for up to 2 weeks.

Cheddar, Apple, and Whole-Grain-Mustard Panini

▶ **Yield:** 4 panini

Especially in autumn, during apple season, you're bound to have all the ingredients on hand to pull together these simple panini. The flavors are tangy, buttery, and a touch sweet—comfort in sandwich form.

1. Heat the panini press to medium-high heat.

2. *For each sandwich:* Spread butter on two slices of bread to flavor the outside of the sandwich. Flip over both slices and spread a thin layer of mustard on the other sides. Top one slice with cheese, a single layer of apples, and more cheese. Close the sandwich with the other slice of bread, buttered-side up.

3. Grill two panini at a time, with the lid closed, until the cheese is melted and the bread is toasted, 4 to 5 minutes.

4 tablespoons (½ stick, or 55 g) butter, at room temperature

8 slices rustic whole-grain bread, sliced from a dense bakery loaf

½ cup (120 g) whole-grain mustard

8 ounces (225 g) sharp cheddar cheese, sliced

1 medium-size apple, ideally a sweet-tart variety such as Gala or Jonagold, cored and thinly sliced

Honey Walnut–Crusted Aged Cheddar Panini

▶ **Yield:** 4 panini

¼ cup finely (30 g) chopped walnuts

4 tablespoons (½ stick, or 55 g) butter, at room temperature

1 tablespoon (20 g) honey

8 slices of rustic white bread, sliced from a dense bakery loaf

8 ounces (225 g) aged sharp cheddar cheese, thinly sliced

A visit to Beecher's Handmade Cheese, a small but renowned shop at Pike Place Market in Seattle, gave me a newfound appreciation for grilled cheese. Their basic grilled cheese sandwich—composed simply of their super-sharp, tangy Flagship cheese panini-grilled between two slices of rustic bread—compelled me to slow things down in my otherwise hectic day and savor every last gooey bite.

The day after I returned home I picked up a block of their cheese from my local grocery store so I could relive the experience on my own grill. I added a honey-walnut crust on the bread to lift the cheese onto a lightly sweet and crunchy pedestal. Any good-quality aged cheddar will work well in this recipe, but if you have the chance to try it with Beecher's, do!

1. Heat the panini press to medium-high heat.

2. In a small bowl, mix the chopped walnuts, butter, and honey until well combined.

3. *For each sandwich:* Spread a layer of honey-walnut butter on two slices of bread. Flip over one slice of bread and top the other side with cheese. Close the sandwich with the other slice of bread, buttered side up.

4. Grill two panini at a time, with the lid closed, until the cheese is melted and the bread is toasted, 4 to 5 minutes.

Cheddar, Bacon, and Apple-Onion Panini

▸ **Yield:** 4 panini

I'm proud to say that I won a sandwich competition with this recipe. It was my concept for the ultimate autumn grilled cheese: sharp aged cheddar and smoky bacon with a sweet and tangy homemade caramelized apple-onion chutney on rye. Luckily, it was the ultimate in the minds—and taste buds—of the contest voters as well.

1. Heat the panini press to medium-high heat.

2. *For each sandwich:* Spread butter on two slices of bread to flavor the outside of the sandwich. Flip over one slice and top the other side with cheese, a few spoonfuls of Carmalized Apple-Onion Chutney, bacon, and more cheese. Close the sandwich with the other slice of bread, buttered side up.

3. Grill two panini at a time, with the lid closed, until the cheese is melted and the bread is toasted, 4 to 5 minutes.

- 4 tablespoons (½ stick, or 55 g) unsalted butter, at room temperature
- 8 slices of rye bread, sliced from a dense bakery loaf
- 8 ounces (225 g) sharp aged cheddar cheese, sliced
- ¾ cup (188 g) Caramelized Apple-Onion Chutney (recipe follows)
- 8 strips of cooked bacon

Caramelized Apple-Onion Chutney

▸ **Yield:** About 2 cups (500 g)

This chutney is especially tasty with sharp-cheddar grilled cheese panini, but it also makes a flavorful condiment for roast pork or chicken.

Heat the butter and olive oil in a large skillet over medium heat. Once the butter melts, add the onions, shallots, and salt and cook, stirring occasionally, until they are tender, about 10 minutes. Add the remaining ingredients and cook until the chutney is golden-brown and caramelized, another 13 to 15 minutes. Refrigerate the chutney in an airtight container for up to 5 days.

- 1 tablespoon (14 g) unsalted butter
- 1 tablespoon (15 ml) extra-virgin olive oil
- 2 medium-size onions, halved and thinly sliced
- 2 tablespoons (20 g) minced shallots
- ½ teaspoon coarse salt
- 2 medium-size Granny Smith apples, peeled, cored, and thinly sliced
- 3 tablespoons (45 ml) cider vinegar
- 1 tablespoon (15 ml) freshly squeezed lemon juice
- 1 tablespoon (15 g) light brown sugar
- ½ teaspoon mustard seeds
- ¼ teaspoon ground allspice
- ⅛ teaspoon freshly ground black pepper

Gruyère, Apples, and Fig Preserves Panini

▶ **Yield:** 4 panini

4 tablespoons (½ stick, or 55 g) butter, at room temperature

8 slices rustic whole-grain bread, sliced from a dense bakery loaf

4 tablespoons (80 g) fig preserves

8 ounces (225 g) Gruyère cheese, thinly sliced

1 Granny Smith apple, cored and thinly sliced

I keep a little file of tasting notes when I come up with new sandwiches. For this, I jotted down "Sweet, savory, and stretchy!" For some reason "stretchy" stands out in my mind as a desirable food trait. It must be the element of fun involved—you pull and pull and the strands of cheese just keep extending into a stringy pile of spirals. And then you get to pick them up and drop them into your mouth. Here's to playing with your food!

1. Heat the panini press to medium-high heat.

2. *For each sandwich:* Spread butter on two slices of bread to flavor the outside of the sandwich. Flip over both slices and spread a layer of fig preserves on the other side of each. To one slice add cheese, apple slices, and more cheese. Close the sandwich with the other slice of bread, buttered side up.

3. Grill two panini at a time, with the lid closed, until the cheese is melted and the bread is toasted, 4 to 5 minutes.

Brie, Basil, Bacon, and Blue Cheese Panini

▶ **Yield:** *4 panini*

Brie, basil, bacon, and blue cheese . . . well, it's just a happy coincidence that all of these ingredients start with "B." They happen to combine into a pretty amazing grilled cheese sandwich.

Even if you're not a fan of blue cheese—I'm speaking to my husband here—you still have got to dab on just a little bit. The tangy flavor borders on sweet amidst the smoky bacon, bright basil, and creamy Brie.

1. Heat the panini press to medium-high heat.

2. *For each sandwich:* Slice off the domed top of a baguette portion to create a flat grilling surface. Split the baguette to create top and bottom halves. Inside the bottom half, lay a thin layer of Brie slices and sprinkle about a tablespoon (8 g) of blue cheese on top. Add 2 basil leaves, 2 bacon strips, more blue cheese, and more Brie. Close the sandwich with the top half.

3. Grill two panini at a time, with the lid closed, until the cheese is melted and the baguettes are toasted, 4 to 5 minutes.

1 French baguette, cut into 4 portions, or 4 mini baguettes

4 ounces (115 g) Brie cheese (with or without the rind), sliced

2 ounces (55 g) crumbled blue cheese

8 fresh basil leaves

8 strips of cooked bacon

Brie and Orange Marmalade Panini

▶ **Yield:** 4 panini

1 multigrain baguette, cut into 4 portions, or 4 mini baguettes

½ cup (160 g) orange marmalade

4 ounces (115 g) Brie cheese (with or without the rind), sliced

I've never seen a baked Brie appetizer survive to the end of a party—it's always the first to go. People love it for good reason. Warm, buttery Brie pairs so naturally with sweet condiments like honey, preserves, and marmalade. The combination also makes a pretty irresistible grilled cheese sandwich. I used orange marmalade in this recipe, but you could easily substitute any other sweet spread that you enjoy with Brie, such as fig preserves or raspberry jam.

1. Heat the panini press to medium-high heat.

2. *For each sandwich:* Slice off the domed top of a baguette portion to create a flat grilling surface. Split the baguette to create top and bottom halves. Spread 1 tablespoon (20 g) marmalade inside both halves. Add a few slices of Brie to the bottom baguette half and close the sandwich with the top half.

3. Grill two panini at a time, with the lid closed, until the cheese is melted and the baguettes are toasted, 5 to 7 minutes.

Spicy Grilled Cheese Sliders

▶ **Yield:** *4 servings*

I learned this little trick from a local pizza place. One of the waiters divulged that the kick of flavor I couldn't get enough of in their pizza was actually a drizzle of chili oil on the crust. It's amazing what a difference the chili oil makes to the pizza—I knew it would be just as enlivening on grilled cheese sandwiches.

To spice things up even more for these sliders, I shred a blend of pepper Jack cheese along with some stretchy mozzarella. Stack up these sliders next to a nice warm mug of tomato bisque.

4 ounces (115 g) shredded pepper Jack cheese (about 1 cup)

4 ounces (115 g) shredded mozzarella cheese (about 1 cup)

1 large sourdough baguette (about 3 inches [7.5 cm] in diameter), sliced crosswise into 16 ½-inch (1.3 cm) thick slices

Chili oil for brushing (see Note)

1. Heat the panini press to medium-high heat.

2. In a medium-size bowl, combine the pepper Jack and mozzarella cheeses. Lay out half of the baguette slices. Drop a few spoonfuls of cheese on each baguette slice. Place the remaining baguette slices on top to form each slider. Brush a little chili oil on top of each slider.

3. Working in batches as needed, grill the sliders, with the lid closed, until the cheese is melted, 3 to 4 minutes.

NOTE: Look for chili oil, a spicy condiment that's been infused with chili peppers, alongside other oils or in the Asian foods section of your grocery store. The amount of heat can vary from brand to brand, so taste it first to gauge how much to use.

Green Goddess Grilled Cheese Panini

▶ **Yield:** 4 to 6 panini

Bursting with bright, fresh green herbs and kicked up with the bold flavors of garlic and anchovies, Green Goddess salad dressing has been making a bit of a comeback in recent years. It was first created at the Palace Hotel in San Francisco back in the 1920s. Now it's again popping up at restaurants and being bottled commercially by major brands. As I toyed with ideas for making green panini for St. Patrick's Day one year, it struck me to invent grilled cheese panini based on this very green classic.

1. Place the garlic and anchovies in a mini food processor and pulse a few times until they're very finely minced, almost a paste (if you don't have a food processor, just mince the ingredients as finely as possible with a knife).

2. Add the lime zest, parsley, tarragon, cilantro, basil, shallot, mustard, and cream cheese and pulse again until well blended. Transfer the mixture to a medium-size bowl and stir in the mozzarella and cheddar cheeses.

3. Heat the panini press to medium-high heat.

4. *For each sandwich:* Spread butter on two slices of bread to flavor the outside of the sandwich. Flip over one slice and spread a generous amount of the cheese mixture on the other side. Close the sandwich with the other slice of bread, buttered side up.

5. Grill two panini at a time, with the lid closed, until the cheese is melted and oozy and the bread is toasted, 5 to 6 minutes.

NOTE: The total number of panini will depend on the size of your bread. Take care not to overfill each sandwich.

1 garlic clove, finely chopped

1 anchovy fillet, finely chopped

Zest of 1 lime (about 1 teaspoon)

3 tablespoons (12 g) chopped fresh flat-leaf parsley

2 tablespoons (8 g) chopped fresh tarragon

2 tablespoons (2 g) chopped fresh cilantro

1 tablespoon (3 g) chopped fresh basil

1 tablespoon (10 g) finely chopped shallot

¼ teaspoon Dijon mustard

2 ounces (55 g) cream cheese, cut into small cubes

4 ounces (115 g) shredded mozzarella cheese (about 1 cup)

4 ounces (115 g) shredded sharp white cheddar cheese (about 1 cup)

4 to 6 tablespoons (55 to 85 g) butter, at room temperature

8 to 12 slices of sourdough bread, sliced from a dense bakery loaf

ON THE MORNING MENU

Breakfast and Brunch on the Panini Press

PANINI

Strawberry, Banana, and Nutella Panini

▶ **Yield:** 4 panini

These sandwiches quickly became some of the most popular on PaniniHappy.com for one main reason: Nutella. To this day, I still feel sneaky whenever I dip into the Nutella jar—it just seems so wrong to eat spreadable chocolate by the spoonful. I even go so far as to store it in the back of my pantry to avoid temptation.

The truth is that I really do love the stuff. And when it's heated up with fresh strawberries and bananas between two slices of buttered and toasted whole-grain bread, it's irresistible! If you're among the many who unabashedly enjoy Nutella for breakfast, this will definitely make for a very happy start to your day.

1. Heat the panini press to medium-high heat.

2. *For each sandwich:* Spread butter on two slices of bread to flavor the outside of the sandwich. Flip over both slices and spread some Nutella on the other side of each. Top one slice with a single layer of strawberries and bananas. Close the sandwich with the other slice of bread, buttered side up.

3. Grill two panini at a time, with the lid closed, until they are heated through and the bread is toasted, 3 to 4 minutes.

4 tablespoons (½ stick, or 55 g) butter, at room temperature

8 slices of rustic whole-grain bread, sliced from a dense bakery loaf

¾ cup (222 g) Nutella chocolate hazelnut spread

4 to 6 strawberries, sliced

1 banana, sliced

Granola-Crusted Pear, Almond Butter, and Honey Panini

▶ **Yield:** 4 panini

We go through a ton of granola at our house, mostly as a healthy, crunchy topping for yogurt parfaits. Did you know that granola also makes a pretty terrific sandwich crust? All you do is crush the granola, mix it with butter, spread it all over the outside of your bread, and grill your sandwiches for an irresistibly crunchy exterior. It's an easy way to take these sweet panini to the next level.

1. Pulse the granola in a food processor until the oats have been cut down to about ⅛-inch (3 mm) bits, but not completely ground up. Mix the chopped granola with the butter until it's well combined.

2. *For each sandwich:* Spread the granola butter on two slices of bread to create the outer crust of the sandwich. Flip over both slices of bread and spread almond butter on each. Top one slice of bread with a layer of pear slices and a drizzle of honey. Close the sandwich with the other slice of bread, buttered side up.

3. Grill two panini at a time, with the lid closed, until the bread is toasted, 3 to 4 minutes.

¼ cup (27 g) granola
4 tablespoons (½ stick, or 55 g) butter, at room temperature
8 slices of rustic white bread, sliced from a dense bakery loaf
½ cup (130 g) almond butter or peanut butter
1 ripe pear or apple, peeled, cored, and sliced
2 teaspoons honey

Blueberry Ricotta Grilled Cheese Panini

▶ **Yield:** 4 panini

¾ cup (188 g) ricotta

2 teaspoons honey, plus more for drizzling

1 teaspoon grated lemon zest

8 thick slices brioche, challah, or other soft enriched bread

½ cup (75 g) fresh blueberries

1 teaspoon chopped fresh mint

They may remind you more of light, sweet blintzes than typical grilled cheese sandwiches, but don't let that stop you from experiencing these panini. Soft and almost fluffy, these sandwiches are one of those rare panini recipes where a softer bread, like thick-cut brioche, is the best accompaniment to the delicate fillings.

1. In a small bowl, mix the ricotta, 2 teaspoons honey, and lemon zest until well combined.

2. Heat the panini press to medium-high heat.

3. *For each sandwich:* Spread a generous layer of the ricotta mixture on one slice of bread. Top the ricotta with blueberries and mint. Add a drizzle of honey and dot on another tablespoon (16 g) of ricotta. Close the sandwich with another slice of bread.

4. If your grill allows you to adjust the height of the upper plate, adjust it so that it rests on top of the bread without pressing it (soft breads like brioche have a tendency to flatten under the weight of the panini press). Grill the panini, two at a time, until the bread is toasted, about 2 minutes.

Bacon, Egg, and Cheddar English Muffin Panini

▶ **Yield:** 4 panini

2 teaspoons butter
4 large eggs
Coarse salt and freshly
    ground black pepper
4 thick English muffins
4 ounces (115 g) sharp
    cheddar cheese, sliced
8 strips of cooked bacon

If I had to choose my single favorite breakfast sandwich, this would have to be it: the classic bacon, egg, and cheese on an English muffin. It's the all-American breakfast in handheld form and it's simply perfect. While I love standard English muffins with all their "nooks and crannies," these sandwiches hold up better on the panini press with brands of muffins that are a bit thicker and denser.

1. One at a time, prepare the omelets. Melt ½ teaspoon of the butter in a small nonstick skillet over medium-low heat. Beat 1 egg very well in a small bowl, season it with salt and pepper, and pour it into the skillet. Once the egg has set slightly, pull in the sides with a rubber spatula to allow the runny egg to flow to the edges of the pan. When the egg is nearly set, carefully lift up one edge with the rubber spatula and fold it in half. Transfer the omelet to a plate and tent it with foil to keep it warm while you prepare the other three omelets in the same manner.

2. Heat the panini press to medium-high heat.

3. *For each sandwich:* Split an English muffin to create top and bottom halves. On the bottom half, layer cheese, an omelet (folded again, if necessary, to fit on the muffin), 2 bacon strips, and more cheese. Close the sandwich with the top English muffin half.

4. Working in batches if necessary, grill the panini, with the lid closed, until the cheese is melted and the muffins are toasted, 4 to 5 minutes.

Monte Cristo Panini

▶ **Yield:** 4 panini

For years, a ham and cheese sandwich was, to me, just that: ham, cheese, and bread (maybe a little mustard, definitely not mayo). If there's one thing I've learned since starting PaniniHappy.com, it's that there are about a million and one ways to make ham and cheese. My favorite of them all, thus far, has got to be the Monte Cristo. This is the savory French toast version of ham and cheese, where you dip the bread in an egg batter before grilling and serve the sandwiches with a sprinkling of confectioners' sugar and a side of sweet preserves. Just as with French toast, it's gently crisp on the outside and pleasantly spongy on the inside. When I'm feeling particularly "gourmet," I make these with prosciutto and Gruyère, but regular sliced deli ham and Swiss cheese work just as well.

2 tablespoons (40 g) honey
2 tablespoons (30 g) Dijon mustard
2 large eggs
¼ cup (60 ml) milk
½ teaspoon coarse salt
¼ teaspoon freshly ground black pepper
⅛ teaspoon ground nutmeg
8 slices of rustic white bread, sliced from a dense bakery loaf
8 ounces (225 g) Gruyère or Swiss cheese, sliced
8 ounces (225 g) sliced prosciutto or ham
Confectioners' sugar, for dusting
Strawberry or raspberry preserves, for serving

1. Heat the panini press to medium-high heat.

2. In a small bowl, mix the honey with the mustard until they're well combined.

3. In a shallow bowl, whisk together the eggs, milk, salt, pepper, and nutmeg.

4. *For each sandwich:* Spread a few teaspoons (18 to 24 g) of honey mustard on two slices of bread. On one slice of bread, layer cheese, prosciutto, and more cheese. Close the sandwich with the other slice of bread, honey mustard side down.

5. Just before grilling, dip both sides of the sandwich into the egg batter. Allow the bread to sit and soak up the liquid for several seconds.

6. Grill two panini at a time, with the lid closed, until the cheese is melted and the sandwich is browned and cooked through, about 5 minutes.

7. Dust the sandwiches with confectioners' sugar and serve them with preserves.

Egg White Omelet Panino with Spinach, Feta, and Sun-Dried Tomatoes

▶ **Yield:** 1 panino (see Note)

Beyond the coffee—mostly decaf for me these days—I've become a fan of the food at that popular Seattle-based coffee chain with the green and white logo. One item in particular, a spinach and feta breakfast wrap made with egg whites, is so flavorful and satisfying that I easily forget that it's classed as a healthier option. The egg whites pack a lot of protein, feta is naturally low in fat, and the green, leafy spinach is loaded with nutrients. One day I ventured to make my own version of this fabulous wrap and it came together in a snap.

3 large egg whites
Coarse salt and freshly ground black pepper
2 slices of sourdough or other rustic white bread, sliced from a dense bakery loaf
¼ cup (8 g) loosely packed baby spinach
3 oil-packed sun-dried tomatoes, thinly sliced
1 ounce (28 g) crumbled feta cheese

1. Spray a little nonstick cooking spray in a small skillet and heat it over medium-high heat.

2. Meanwhile, in a large bowl, whisk the egg whites until they're frothy. Season them with salt and pepper. Pour the egg whites into the skillet and let them cook until they're set on the bottom, about 1 minute. With a spatula, carefully lift up one side and fold it over, creating a half-moon shape. Continue cooking the omelet, flipping after another minute or so, until it's cooked through and set. Slide the omelet onto a plate and tent it with foil to keep it warm while you assemble the sandwich.

3. Heat the panini press to medium-high heat.

4. Create a little bed of baby spinach on one slice of bread and lay your egg white omelet on top of it. Arrange the sun-dried tomato slices on the omelet and sprinkle the feta on top. Close the sandwich with the other slice of bread.

5. Grill the sandwich, with the lid closed, until the cheese is softened and the bread is toasted, 4 to 5 minutes.

NOTE: You can easily scale up this recipe to make more servings; just be sure to cook the egg white omelets one at a time.

Caramel Apple–Stuffed French Toast

▶ **Yield:** 4 servings

CARAMELIZED APPLES
3 tablespoons (45 g) butter
2 tablespoons (26 g) sugar
1 teaspoon ground
 cinnamon
A pinch of coarse salt
2 medium-size apples
 (about 1 pound, or
 455 g), peeled, cored,
 and sliced (I like to use
 Gala)
⅓ cup (80 ml) heavy cream

FRENCH TOAST
4 slices day-old challah,
 each about
 1½ inches (3.8 cm) thick
4 large eggs
1⅓ cups (315 ml) milk
¼ cup (50 g) sugar
½ teaspoon ground
 cinnamon
¼ teaspoon pure vanilla
 extract
1 recipe Toasted Pecan
 Maple Syrup
 (recipe follows)

I was leafing through the pages of my favorite specialty cookware catalog when my eyes stopped on a photo of the most gorgeous, thick-cut, caramelized banana–stuffed French toast, created by chef Bryan Voltaggio. Better yet, it was grilled on a panini press! I, of course, had no choice but to try it out and I, of course, loved it.

Here, I've adapted Chef Voltaggio's recipe to feature caramelized cinnamon apples stuffed within the fluffy challah French toast. Once you drizzle the praline-like toasted pecan maple syrup down those lightly crisp grilled ridges—we're talking dessert for breakfast. Tell your family to have a little patience while you prepare this special-occasion French toast. It will be well worth the wait.

1. *Caramelized Apples:* Melt the butter in a large skillet over medium heat. Stir in the sugar, cinnamon, salt, and apples. Cook, stirring frequently, until the apples are brown and tender and a deep brown caramel forms, 7 to 10 minutes. Add the cream and simmer until the sauce thickens slightly, about 2 minutes. Transfer the apples to a medium-size bowl and let them cool.

2. *French Toast:* Using a small, sharp knife, create a pocket in each bread slice by cutting a 2-inch (5 cm) long slit in the crust on one side of the bread and continuing to cut three-quarters of the way through the bread. Stuff the pockets with a few of the apple slices (this is a messy business!). Reserve the rest of the apples for serving.

3. Heat the panini press to medium-high heat.

4. In a large shallow bowl, whisk together the eggs, milk, sugar, cinnamon, and vanilla. Soak two of the bread slices for about 2 minutes per side.

5. Place the eggy bread on the panini press and, if possible, adjust the top plate so that it lightly presses the bread. Grill the toast until it's browned and cooked through, about 5 minutes. Transfer the toast to a plate and tent it with foil to keep it warm while you soak and grill the remaining two bread slices. Serve the French toast with more Caramelized Apples and the Toasted Pecan Maple Syrup.

Toasted Pecan Maple Syrup

▶ **Yield:** About 1 cup (245 g)

A special French toast deserves a special syrup to go along with it. It takes less than 10 minutes to give ordinary maple syrup a nutty boost with butter-toasted pecans.

1 tablespoon (14 g) unsalted butter
½ cup (55 g) chopped pecans
A pinch of coarse salt
¾ cup (175 ml) pure maple syrup

Melt the butter in a small skillet or saucepan over medium heat and cook until it's lightly browned, a few minutes. Add the pecans and cook, stirring occasionally, until the pecans are lightly toasted and aromatic, about 3 minutes. Stir in the salt and maple syrup. Turn up the heat to medium-high and cook the syrup until it's slightly thickened, about 2 minutes. Transfer the syrup to a bowl and keep it warm while you prepare the French toast. If you've made the syrup in advance, reheat it on the stove or in the microwave.

Ham, Egg, and Cheddar Breakfast Crêpes

▶ **Yield:** 4 rolled crêpes

CRÊPES
½ cup (63 g) all-purpose
    flour
½ cup (120 ml) milk
¼ cup (60 ml) lukewarm
    water
2 large eggs
2 tablespoons (28 g) butter,
    melted, plus 2 teaspoons
    (9 g) butter for the pan
½ teaspoon coarse salt

OMELETS
Butter for the pan, if
    necessary
4 large eggs
Coarse salt and freshly
    ground black pepper

FILLING
4 ounces (115 g) cheddar
    cheese, sliced
4 ounces (115 g) sliced
    ham

OPTIONAL GARNISH
Oil-packed sun-dried toma-
    toes, plus some of the oil
    from the jar

I first made these crêpes for a Valentine's Day post on PaniniHappy.com. The holiday fell on a weekend that year, which meant I could pull off a special family breakfast for the occasion: an omelet, sliced ham, and cheddar cheese rolled in a savory crêpe and grilled on the panini press. It sounds like a lot of work, but in reality the crêpes and omelets each take only a few minutes to make. The sun-dried tomato puree, aside from looking cute on the plate in its heart shape, adds a nice sweetness to the crepes.

Make It Ahead: You can prepare and refrigerate the crêpe batter up to 2 days ahead of time. Also, once you've cooked the crêpes, you can store them, cooled, separated by waxed paper, and wrapped airtight, in the freezer for up to 1 month. Defrost the crepes either in the microwave or overnight in the refrigerator.

1. *Crêpes:* Blend the flour, milk, water, eggs, 2 tablespoons (28 ml) melted butter, and salt in a blender or food processor until you have a smooth batter. Transfer the batter to a pitcher or liquid measuring cup. Let the batter stand, covered, at room temperature for 30 minutes.

2. Melt ½ teaspoon butter in a small nonstick skillet over medium heat. Give the batter a quick stir and pour about 2 tablespoons (28 ml) into the pan, swirling the pan around to create a very thin, even crêpe. Cook the crêpe until the top is set and the underside is golden brown, 30 to 60 seconds. Carefully flip the crêpe with a spatula or your fingers and cook the other side until it's lightly browned as well. Transfer the crêpe to a plate lined with waxed paper.

3. Cook the remaining crêpes in this manner, remembering to butter the pan and stir the batter before making each one. As each crêpe is done, add it to the stack, using waxed paper in between each one to prevent sticking.

4. *Omelets:* Make the omelets one at a time, ideally just prior to rolling them into the crêpes. In a small bowl beat 1 egg and season it with salt and pepper to taste. Pour the egg into the same small nonstick skillet that you used for the crêpes (melt more butter in the pan, if needed) and cook until the top is set and the underside is lightly browned. Flip it with a spatula and cook the other side until it's cooked through.

5. Heat the panini press to medium heat.

6. *Filling:* Place one crêpe on a work surface. Place one omelet on top of the crêpe (the omelet should be about the same size as the crêpe). Layer cheese and ham on top of the omelet. Carefully roll up the crêpe and place it, seam side down, on the panini press.

7. Grill two crêpes at a time, with the lid closed, until the cheese is melted and golden grill marks appear, about 2 minutes.

8. *Optional Garnish:* Puree sun-dried tomatoes and a small amount of the oil in a blender or mini food processor to create a paste. Spoon the puree into a small plastic bag, snip off one corner of the bag, and pipe the puree in a heart shape—or any other design you like—onto the plate alongside each crêpe.

A LITTLE SOMETHING SWEET

Dessert on the Panini Press

Brie, Nutella, and Basil Panini

▶ **Yield:** 4 panini

I have yet to meet someone who doesn't flinch uncomfortably when I mention the concept of chocolate, Brie, and basil panini. I have to admit, I had that same "uhh . . . no thanks" reaction when I first watched Giada De Laurentiis grill these sandwiches on TV. But I was also intrigued. I gave them a try one day and—wow!—Giada was right, it's a magical combination! The key ingredient, to my surprise, turned out to be the basil. It adds just the right amount of fresh, herbal flavor, much like mint (which we all know pairs very well with chocolate).

For my version, I've brought in Nutella to add the flavor of hazelnuts along with the chocolate. Bread is more of a supporting player in these panini than the star, but I'll tell you what, some buttery brioche is the perfect complement for these rich dessert sandwiches if you've got it!

4 ounces (115 g) Brie cheese (with or without the rind), sliced

8 slices brioche, each about ½ inch (1.3 cm) thick

8 fresh basil leaves

½ cup (148 g) Nutella or other chocolate hazelnut spread

1. Heat the panini press to medium-high heat.

2. *For each sandwich:* Lay a few slices of Brie on one slice of brioche and top them with 2 basil leaves. Spread 2 tablespoons (37 g) Nutella on another slice of bread and place it on top of the basil, Nutella side down, to close the sandwich.

3. Grill two panini at a time, with the lid closed, until the cheese is melted and the bread is toasted, about 2 minutes.

Apple Pie Panini

▶ **Yield:** *4 panini*

What about a sandwich that tastes just like apple pie?" my sister Julie suggested to me in an email one day. I stopped what I was doing and, suddenly, I could think about nothing else besides apple pie panini. How dreamy would that be—tart apple slices layered with honey-whipped mascarpone on cinnamon raisin bread with a brown sugar crust on top? Well, here's the simple recipe for that dessert sandwich dream come true.

1. Either in a small bowl with a whisk or in a mini food processor, whip the mascarpone and honey together until well combined and fluffy.

2. Heat the panini press to medium-high heat.

3. *For each sandwich:* Spread butter on two slices of bread to flavor the outside of the sandwich. Flip over both slices of bread and spread 1 tablespoon (15 g) sweetened mascarpone on each. Top one slice of bread with a layer of apples and close the sandwich with the other slice, buttered side up. Sprinkle some brown sugar on top.

4. Grill two panini at a time, with the lid closed, until the fillings are warmed and the bread is toasted, with a sweet crust, 3 to 5 minutes.

½ cup (120 g) mascarpone cheese

2 teaspoons honey

4 tablespoons (½ stick, or 55 g) butter, at room temperature

8 slices of cinnamon raisin bread, sliced from a dense bakery loaf

1 Granny Smith or other firm apple, cored and thinly sliced

2 tablespoons (30 g) light brown sugar

Strawberries, Basil, and Lemon Curd Pound Cake Tartines

▶ **Yield:** 4 tartines

Think of these easy-to-make tartines the next time you're looking for a crowd-pleasing dessert to bring to a spring or summer potluck. Not only do these open-faced pound cake sandwiches look pretty on display, they're incredibly quick to assemble. Make a few extras to keep at home because you'll be leaving the party with an empty tray!

1. Heat the panini press to medium-high heat.

2. Grill the pound cake slices, with the lid closed, until they're toasted and grill marks appear, 1 to 2 minutes.

3. Transfer the slices to a serving platter. Top each slice with a generous layer of Lemon Curd, strawberry slices, and basil.

4 slices pound cake, each about ½ inch (1.3 cm) thick
½ cup (125 g) Lemon Curd, purchased or homemade (page 171)
½ cup (85 g) sliced strawberries
1 tablespoon (20 g) torn fresh basil leaves

Fluffernutter Panini

▶ **Yield:** 4 panini

4 tablespoons(60 g)
    unsalted butter, at room
    temperature
2 tablespoons (28 ml)
    sugar
2 teaspoons ground
    cinnamon
A pinch of coarse salt
8 slices of white bread, each
    about 1 inch thick
½ cup of peanut butter
½ cup of Marshmallow
    Fluff or other marsh-
    mallow crème
¼ cup (55 g) of Candied
    Peanuts (recipe follows)

I get why the people of Massachusetts sought to have the Fluffernutter—a peanut butter and marshmallow crème sandwich concoction—designated as their official state sandwich. But in reality, these things ought to be illegal, they're so decadent. Well, far be it from me to judge . . . or deny that this sandwich sounded pretty appealing to me. So I went ahead and dressed up my grilled version with nuggets of crunchy candied peanuts dispersed throughout the sandwich and added a cinnamon-sugar crust. Go big, right?

1. In a small bowl, mix the butter, sugar, cinnamon, and salt until they're well combined.

2. Heat the panini press to medium-high heat.

3. *For each sandwich:* Spread a layer of cinnamon-sugar butter on two slices of bread. Flip them over and spread a generous layer of peanut butter on one slice and a good amount of Marshmallow Fluff on the other. Scatter a small handful of candied peanuts over the peanut butter and close the sandwich with the other slice of bread, marshmallow side down.

4. Grill two panini at a time, with the lid closed, until the Marshmallow Fluff is melted and the bread is toasted, 2 to 3 minutes.

Candied Peanuts

▶ **Yield:** 1 cup (230 g)

If you find yourself with extra candied peanuts on hand, save them to top Grown-Up Grilled Banana Splits (page 324). Or keep them around for a sweet snack.

¼ **cup sugar**
¼ **teaspoon coarse salt**
1 **tablespoon (15 ml) water**
½ **teaspoon pure vanilla extract**
1 **cup unsalted roasted peanuts**

1. Lay out a large sheet of aluminum foil and coat it with nonstick cooking spray. Set aside.

2. Combine all of the ingredients in a large, heavy-bottomed skillet over medium-high heat. Cook, stirring constantly, as the mixture goes from syrupy to dry and sandy and finally to a deep brown, smooth caramel stage, 10 to 12 minutes. Carefully pour the candied peanuts onto the prepared foil and allow them to cool for 5 minutes. Transfer the peanuts to an airtight container, breaking the candy apart if needed, and store them at room temperature for up to 2 weeks.

Grilled Pears with Honey-Whipped Greek Yogurt and Toasted Almonds

▶ **Yield:** *4 servings*

When fresh pear halves begin to sear on a hot panini grill, it smells as if someone is stirring up homemade caramel nearby. I like to drop these candy-like pears into a martini glass with cold, creamy Greek yogurt that I've whipped with a little honey and vanilla. A sprinkling of toasted almonds and an extra drizzle of honey are all that's needed to turn these simple ingredients into something special.

1 cup (230 g) plain whole-milk Greek yogurt

2 tablespoons (40 g) honey, plus more for drizzling

½ teaspoon pure vanilla extract

¼ cup (36 g) blanched whole almonds

4 ripe pears, such as D'Anjou or Bosc

1 tablespoon (14 g) butter, melted

1. Whip the yogurt, honey, and vanilla in a blender or mini food processor, or with an electric mixer, until it's creamy, smooth, and shiny, about 2 minutes. Transfer it to a small bowl, cover, and refrigerate while you prepare the other ingredients.

2. Heat the oven or toaster oven to 350°F (180°C, or gas mark 4). Spread the almonds on a baking sheet and bake until they're fragrant, about 5 minutes. Keep your eye on them to make sure they don't burn!

3. Heat the panini press to high.

4. Halve each pear lengthwise and remove the core (an easy way is to scoop out the core with a teaspoon). Brush a little melted butter on the cut sides.

5. In batches, place the pear halves, cut sides down, on the grill and close the lid so that it rests gently on top of the pears. Grill until dark grill marks appear and you can smell the aroma of burnt caramel, about 3 minutes.

6. Transfer the pear halves, cut sides up, to individual bowls or martini glasses. Top with a few dollops of the honey-whipped yogurt, sprinkle on a few toasted almonds, and drizzle with honey.

Grown-up Grilled Banana Splits

▶ **Yield:** 4 servings

4 very ripe bananas (with lots of brown spots)

4 scoops of vanilla ice cream

3 tablespoons (27 g) chopped salted dry-roasted peanuts

Something pretty incredible happens when you grill a super-ripe banana in its peel. An already sweet treat turns near candy-like as the pulp softens, the juices are released, and it caramelizes inside the peel. Once you break it open, all you need is a spoon (and maybe a scoop of ice cream and some salted peanuts) to enjoy a very simple and—dare I say, grown-up—version of a banana split. If you're feeling very decadent, sub in my Candied Peanuts (see page 165) for the plain peanuts.

1. Heat the panini press to medium-high heat.

2. Set the bananas directly on the grill (in their peels) and close the lid. Grill the bananas until they feel rather soft when you give them a poke, about 8 minutes. You'll start to hear sizzling as the moisture from inside the bananas seeps through the peel.

3. Using tongs, take the bananas off the grill and transfer them to serving plates or bowls.

4. Slide a sharp knife down the center of each banana and peel back the banana peel to expose the soft, hot pulp, which should be swimming in its own caramel. Dollop on a scoop of vanilla ice cream and sprinkle the chopped salted peanuts over the top. Enjoy the whole hot-and-cold, sweet-and-salty dessert right out of the banana peel.

Grilled Apple Turnovers

▶ **Yield:** 8 turnovers

This is an updated version of the very first non-panini recipe I ever posted on PaniniHappy.com. I guess I figured out early on that there was more to this panini press machine than just sandwiches. Lots of familiar foods could be prepared just as well—perhaps even faster and better—on a panini press.

Oven-baked apple turnovers are always a treat. But if you grill them, the resulting ridges give you the excuse to fill those valleys with vanilla ice cream.

Make It Ahead: If you'd like to grill just a few turnovers at a time, you can wrap any assembled, uncooked turnovers tightly in plastic wrap and store them in the refrigerator for 2 to 3 days until you're ready to grill them.

1. In a medium-size bowl, toss the apple slices with the lemon juice. Add the sugar, flour, cinnamon, nutmeg, salt, and cardamom (if you're using it) and toss to coat the apples.

2. Heat the panini press to medium-high heat (if your grill has a temperature setting, set it to 400°F [200°C]).

3. On a lightly floured surface, roll out each puff pastry sheet into a 12-inch (30 c) square. Divide each square into four 6-inch (15 cm) squares.

4. Spoon 6 or 7 apple slices onto the center of each pastry square.

5. In a small bowl, whisk the egg and water together to make an egg wash. One pastry square at a time, brush a little egg wash along the edges of the square and fold it over diagonally to form a triangle. Press the edges together with your fingers and then crimp them with a fork to seal them.

6. Carefully place two turnovers on the grill. Lower the lid until it's very lightly touching them (if your press allows you to fix the height so that the upper plate hovers about ¼ inch [6 mm] above the turnovers, that's even better). As the turnovers bake they'll puff up and make contact with the upper plate—you want to give them a little room to expand. Grill until the pastry is puffed, golden, and crisp on the outside, about 12 minutes. Repeat this step for the remaining 6 turnovers.

7. Serve the turnovers hot with a scoop of ice cream on top, running down into those crinkly pastry ridges.

3 medium-size apples (about 1½ pounds, or 680 g), a combination of sweet and tart, such as Gala and Granny Smith, peeled, cored, and thinly sliced

3 tablespoons (45 ml) freshly squeezed lemon juice

2 tablespoons (26 g) sugar

1 tablespoon (8 g) all-purpose flour

½ teaspoon ground cinnamon

⅛ teaspoon ground nutmeg

A pinch of coarse salt

A pinch of ground cardamom (optional)

1 package (17.3 ounces, or 485 g) of frozen puff pastry sheets, thawed

1 large egg

1 tablespoon (15 ml) water

Ice cream, for serving

Grilled Angel Food Cake with Lemon Curd

▶ **Yield:** 4 servings

8 slices angel food cake, each about 1 inch (2.5 cm) thick (see Note)
1 cup (250 g) Lemon Curd, purchased or homemade (recipe follows)
½ pint (about ¾ cup, or 95 g) fresh raspberries

Something really cool happens when you grill angel food cake: the outside gets ever-so-gently crisped and practically dissolves on your tongue like cotton candy. It transforms an otherwise average, store-bought cake into something far more appealing—especially when you top it with some sweet-tart homemade Lemon Curd.

1. Heat the panini press to high heat.

2. In batches, place the angel food cake slices on the grill. Close the lid so that the upper plate is resting on the cake without pressing it. Grill the cake slices until they're toasted and grill marks appear, about 1 minute. Alternatively, leave the grill open and grill the cake slices for about 90 seconds per side.

3. Serve the grilled angel food cake with a few spoonfuls of Lemon Curd and some fresh raspberries.

NOTE: If you bake your own angel food cake from scratch, save the yolks to make the lemon curd.

Lemon Curd

▶ **Yield:** About 1½ cups (375 g)

Chocolate lovers have their Nutella. If you're a lemon lover, then homemade lemon curd needs to be part of your repertoire. The silky-smooth citrus spread is a terrific topper for treats like angel food cake and pound cake and also makes an easy layer cake filling. It takes a little effort to make your own homemade lemon curd but, as with so many things, it tastes way better than store-bought.

5 large egg yolks
¾ cup (150 g) sugar
2 tablespoons (12 g) finely grated lemon zest
⅓ cup (80 ml) freshly squeezed lemon juice
5 tablespoons (70 g) butter, cubed and chilled

1. Fill a medium-size saucepan with an inch (2.5 cm) of water and bring it to a simmer over medium-high heat (or, if you have a double boiler, heat an inch [2.5 cm] of water in the lower saucepan).

2. Meanwhile, whisk together the egg yolks and sugar in a medium-size heatproof bowl (or the upper saucepan of your double boiler) until smooth. Whisk in the lemon zest and juice until the mixture is smooth.

3. Once the water is simmering, turn down the heat to low and place the bowl on top of the saucepan; the bowl should not touch the water (if you're using a double boiler, assemble the upper and lower saucepans). Whisk the egg mixture continually until it thickens, about 15 minutes. It should be thick enough to coat the back of a wooden spoon.

4. Remove the bowl or upper saucepan from the heat and stir in one cube of butter at a time, incorporating each cube before adding the next. If you're using a double boiler, transfer the curd to a bowl. If you're not serving the curd immediately, press a layer of plastic wrap on the surface of the curd to prevent a skin from forming and refrigerate until you're ready to use it.

5. The lemon curd will thicken quite a bit in the refrigerator. To restore it to a spoonable consistency, set your bowl of curd inside a larger bowl. Fill the larger bowl with enough hot water to rise about halfway up the sides of the bowl of curd. Give the curd a stir every few minutes, refreshing the larger bowl with new hot water, until the curd is soft enough to serve. It will stay fresh in the refrigerator for up to 2 weeks.

About the Author

Kathy Strahs is the creator of the popular blog Panini Happy (paninihappy.com), which Babble.com has named as one of the Top 100 Mom Food Blogs for the past four years. A former marketer with a Stanford MBA, Kathy traded in her corporate career to pursue her passion for cooking in 2008. Her innovative recipes and mouthwatering food photography have since been featured in *The Wall Street Journal*, *Pillsbury Magazine*, *San Diego Family Magazine*, and the Associated Press, and on the New York Times, PBS, The Huffington Post, Saveur, and TLC websites. She is also a frequent cooking contest judge, including for the Grilled Cheese Invitational in Los Angeles and the World Food Championships in Las Vegas. She has written *The Ultimate Panini Press Cookbook*, *The 8X8 Cookbook*, and *The Lemonade Stand Cookbook*. She lives in in the San Francisco Bay Area with her husband and their two children.

About the Photographer

Ellen Callaway is a professional food and product photographer. For more than 20 years, her career has spanned a diverse scope of projects from cookbooks and advertising to packaging.

Ellen also proudly created an advertising campaign to make waste diversion look fun and informative called Recycled Beauty. In 2015, the photo series won a highly acclaimed Hatch Award. Recycled Beauty's publicity ranged from an interviewe by Boston's *Chronicle* news program to a feature article in UK's *Resource* magazine.

In her free time, she enjoys hiking, biking, yoga and obsessing over inconsequential details.

About the Food Stylist

Joy Howard is a food stylist and recipe developer whose work has appeared in numerous cookbooks, magazines, and advertising campaigns. She writes a column on family cooking for *EatingWell*, and lives in New England with her husband and daughters.

Index